What a Story!

Anthology

SERIES EDITORS
Margaret Iveson
Samuel Robinson

EDITORIAL CONSULTANT
Alan Simpson

LITERATURE CONSULTANT
Rivka Cranley

TEACHER CONSULTANTS
Flora Miller
Eldred Barnes

PRENTICE HALL CANADA INC.

ISBN 0-13-020132-4
© 1993 by Prentice-Hall Canada Inc., Scarborough, Ontario

Anthologists: David Friend, Linda Sheppard
Researchers: Monika Croydon, Catherine Rondina

A Ligature Book
Cover Illustration: Phillip Singer

Canadian Cataloguing in Publication Data
Main entry under title:

What a Story!: anthology

(MultiSource)
ISBN 0-13-020132-4

1. Storytelling–Literary collections. 2. Folk
literature. 3. Children's literature. I. Iveson, Margaret L., 1948–   .
II. Robinson, Sam, 1937–   . III. Series.
PZ5.W5 1993   j808.83   C92–095395–6

Printed and bound in Canada

6 7 8 9 FP 02 01 00 99

The universe is made of stories,
not of atoms.

MURIEL RUKEYSER
(1913–1980)
AMERICAN POET

Contents

The Golden Carp

A Chinese folk tale

At the foot of a soaring mountain, there once lived a tribe of people whose chieftain was known as Cave Lord Wu. He was called by this name for he had chosen to make a home for his two wives within the rocky vastness of a large, high-domed cave.

It was Wu's misfortune that his first wife died shortly after giving birth to a baby girl. From an early age it was evident that the girl, named Ye Syan, was endowed with grace and charm. Gentle of nature and kind of heart, she was dearly loved by her father who saw in her all the admirable qualities of his departed wife.

Destiny did not decree that Wu have a long life. Well before Ye Syan reached marriageable age, he sickened and lapsed into a lethargy from which he could not be roused. All the healing herbs gave him little relief, and all the sacrifices offered to bring about his recovery were useless.

Within a week of the onset of his illness, he was dead, leaving Ye Syan in the care of his second wife.

Now that Wu was gone, Ye Syan was at the mercy of her stepmother, a mean, jealous woman. She had long resented Wu's favoritism toward Ye Syan while he ignored her own daughter, an unattractive, dull girl. Wu's death left the stepmother free to take out her bitterness by mistreating Ye Syan without fear of interference from anyone.

Her own daughter was given easy tasks to perform and kept close to home, while Ye Syan was assigned the most unpleasant, arduous chores. Daily, in fair weather or foul, the stepmother would send her out to gather firewood in the higher mountain forests or to lug back buckets of drinking water from distant streams.

On one such errand, Ye Syan happened upon a lake fed by underground springs. As she was about to dip her bucket into the mirror-clear water, she was attracted by a sudden flash of color. It was a tiny fish, no longer than her pinky. Scooping it up, she watched with fascination as it swam round and round inside one of her wooden buckets. How she longed to take it home! The little fish would be a friend when she was lonely, and a comfort when she was abused. Her stepmother was sure to disapprove, but Ye Syan decided there and then to keep it as a pet. She hitched the two buckets full of water to her carrying pole. Unmindful of the heavy weight across her back, half walking, half running, she managed to arrive home without spilling a drop.

Before entering the cave, she transferred her precious fish to an old basin, and thereafter kept it hidden, tucked out of sight. Each day she secretly fed it a few grains of rice from her own bowl, and each day she saw it become longer and more beautiful.

With bright orange fins and a lacy fantail, it soon outgrew the basin, and Ye Syan realized that her fish needed more space. Taking care not to be seen by her stepmother, she was able to carry it, undetected, out of the cave. She took it to a nearby pond, where, within a short time, it reached full size.

Whenever Ye Syan came to the pond, her wonderful fish would surface and flash its fiery fins as if to greet her. Then it would twist sideways, jump straight up into the air, and splash back into the water. As long as she remained there, it entertained her with its playful antics.

The stepmother's curiosity was aroused when she noticed that Ye Syan was spending a great deal of time near the pond. "That lazy wastrel of a girl, idling away hours better given to useful work," she complained. "I'll soon find out what she is up to."

When Ye Syan left the cave that evening, her stepmother followed her. Hidden behind a scraggly bush, she witnessed a strange spectacle. As Ye Syan neared the edge of the pond, a brilliant orange fish with glassy, bulging eyes emerged from the water. It rested its scaly head on the gravel bank and permitted Ye Syan to stroke it. With a wave of its lacy tail, it turned and plopped back into the pool.

"So that is how she spends her time, in useless play with a fish!" the stepmother fumed. "This I will not tolerate! Besides, that fish will make a delicious meal. I must have it."

Several times thereafter the determined woman came to the pond and waited patiently, but in vain. The fish never showed itself. Disappointed, she would leave empty-handed to return again and again for naught. During the ensuing days she could think of nothing else but how to catch the fish.

Ye Syan came home later than usual one day, tired and footsore, having carried a heavy load of kindling from a far-off woodland. She steeled herself against the usual scolding she expected. Instead, her stepmother greeted her with disarming kindness.

"You dear girl, how hard you have been working," she cooed. "Because you are not lazy and do your chores without complaining, you deserve a reward. See, I have made you a new blouse. Do try it on and give me the old one you are wearing. I shall put it in the rag pile, for it is too shabby to be worth mending."

Ye Syan did not comprehend the change in her step-mother's attitude. Nevertheless, she accepted her offer with a great sense of relief. "Perhaps," she dared to hope, "my life will not be so hard from now on."

The blouse, with its embroidered neck and narrow sleeves, was very becoming. Ye Syan was happier than she had been in all the time since her father's death.

The following morning she was sent off as usual to fetch the day's supply of drinking water.

"I have learned of a spring that has the sweetest and clearest water to be found anywhere," explained her step-mother. "To reach it you must follow the path that winds to the top of the mountain. It is a long distance to go, and you may need to rest along the way. Do not worry if you return later than usual. I shall keep your supper warm."

Within moments after Ye Syan left the cave the scheming stepmother changed into Ye Syan's old clothes, concealing a knife in her waistband. So anxious was she to reach the pond, she almost tripped in her haste to get there. Out of breath, she sat down at the water's edge, when, to her amazement, the fish appeared at her feet. Quick as lightning she pulled it from the water, lopped off its head, and carried it back to her cave home. A pot of simmering fish broth soon filled the air with a delicious aroma. The stepmother and her daughter feasted on the tasty fish to the last savory morsel.

"I shall bury the fishbones in the dunghill," the stepmother said to her daughter. "No one will ever find them there."

Tired from her unusually long walk, Ye Syan returned to find only a bowl of cold rice for her evening meal. Her stepmother spoke not a word, and her stepsister sat fidgeting with her fingers. Ye Syan ate in silence, washed the rice bowl, and, as was her custom, rushed to the pond to visit with her pet. For the first time ever, the fish failed to greet her. Though she called to it repeatedly, the water's surface remained unruffled. She scanned every inch of the pond till her eyes ached. That evening and the next and the next, Ye Syan came to the pond, praying that her fish would return. Each time, she threw grains of rice into the water to tempt it with food, but her friend did not appear. At last, overwhelmed with a sense of loss, she burst into tears. For a long time, she sat near the pond, sick at heart and weeping.

By this time it had turned quite dark. Ye Syan stood up and brushed the soil from her clothes. She had not noticed the bent old stranger leaning on a cane, watching her from the shadows.

"Dry your tears, my child," he said. "The evil deed is done. The fish was killed by your stepmother. You will find its bones in the dunghill. Dig them out and keep them always. Wherever fortune may lead, they will serve you well."

Before Ye Syan could open her lips to reply, the stranger was gone.

The day of a great festival was at hand. In cave homes tunneled into the hillsides and in huts that dotted the valleys, people prepared for the celebration. They looked forward to seeing richly costumed dancers perform to the beat of drums and the clash of cymbals. They would watch acrobats and mummers entertain with acts of daring and pantomime. All manner of delicacies would be offered to please the eye and tempt the appetite. It was the one time in the entire year when people could cease their daily labors and lose themselves in the gaiety of the festivities.

"You will remain at home to guard the fruit orchard," Ye Syan's stepmother declared while she and her daughter readied themselves for the grand occasion. On the way out the door, arrayed in their gaudiest dresses, the stepmother hurled a parting warning at Ye Syan. "When we return, if a single piece of fruit is missing, you will pay dearly!"

Ye Syan often brooded over the unfair treatment she suffered at the hands of her stepmother. For the most part she accepted her lot with resignation. Now to be kept from attending the festival was a cruelty hard to bear. Recalling the stranger's talk about the fishbones, she decided to put them to the test, but so great was her gloom she doubted they would be of any help to her.

With great care, Ye Syan took the fishbones from their hiding place. Then, covering her face with her hands, she made a silent wish.

When she opened her eyes, all about her was a soft mist. Suddenly, a beam of intense light pierced the grayness and shone down on her bed. There, neatly laid out, was a skirt of patterned satin, a matching blouse, and a pair of exquisitely embroidered slippers. Reaching out, she touched them lightly. Yes, they were real! With hesitation, Ye Syan put on the skirt and blouse. The fabric was as soft as gossamer, the colors deep and rich. Then she pulled on the slippers. The transformation was almost miraculous. She looked like a goddess!

A bird released from its cage could not have been happier than Ye Syan as she set off to join the festival celebration. Mingling with the crowds, the extraordinarily beautiful girl became the object of much attention. Along with everyone else, her stepmother and stepsister wondered who she might be.

"Does she not resemble Ye Syan?" the stepsister asked her mother.

"Nonsense," replied the stepmother, dismissing the idea as preposterous. She had told Ye Syan to stay at home and she did not expect to be disobeyed.

Ye Syan joined a ring of spectators that had formed around a group of acrobats. Directly opposite her she spied her stepmother and stepsister. Terrified that they might recognize her, she fled. Frantically pushing her way through the dense crowd of merrymakers, she lost one of her slippers. In her panic, she did not stop to look for it but continued to run, swiftly as a deer, straight toward home.

Upon returning from the festival, the stepmother found Ye Syan asleep in the orchard under a pear tree.

"You see," she said to her daughter, "you were mistaken. The beautiful girl we saw at the festival could not have been Ye Syan."

On the following day, the slipper was found by a poor peasant who sold it for a few coins to an official of the Tuo Huan kingdom.

The Tuo Huan king ruled over a vast territory that included twenty-four islands. Because of his legendary wealth and powerful army, he was envied and feared by all the other weaker tribes. Though he lacked for nothing, he was never content with the riches he had amassed. His craving for more gold, more jewels, even pretty trinkets that caught his fancy, could not be satisfied. The official, anxious to find favor at court, presented the slipper to his king as a gift.

The king was intrigued by the tiny embroidered slipper. "Where is there a maiden," he wondered, "with a foot so dainty? Surely the slipper must belong to a high-born beauty." He resolved to find its owner.

All the young women attached to the palace were required to try on the slipper. Not one of them did it fit. The king then issued a decree that every woman in his kingdom try on his treasured slipper. He sent couriers to every corner of his twenty-four islands, but they all returned without success. Finally, he decided to extend the search beyond his own lands.

The soldier who was dispatched to the area of the cave people never believed he would find the owner of the slipper among its poor inhabitants. When Ye Syan's stepmother led him into her cave dwelling, he was convinced that neither of the two young girls he saw there would be the one he sought. But the king's decree was plain. No one was to be overlooked. The soldier asked Ye Syan's stepsister to try on the slipper first. She tugged and pulled but could not squeeze more than her big toe into it. He handed the slipper to Ye Syan, fully expecting the same results. To the soldier's great surprise, it clung to her foot as though it had been made especially for her.

Still the soldier was unconvinced. It was so unlikely that this ragamuffin would own such a fine slipper. "Give me that slipper," he demanded. "I shall try it on your foot myself." Again the fit was perfect. Still beset by doubts, he asked Ye Syan if she could produce its mate.

From under her straw mattress Ye Syan drew out the other slipper and stepped into it before her open-mouthed stepmother and stepsister.

"You must come with me to the king's palace," the soldier said. "My orders are to bring back the maiden whose foot fits the slipper."

Ye Syan asked for time to change her clothes. Quickly, she threw off her old worn rags. She returned wearing her lovely new outfit. The stepmother, astonished by the change in her appearance, recognized that the attractive girl she had seen at the festival was indeed Ye Syan. Her jealousy and wrath knew no bounds, but she could only look on helplessly. Escorted by the king's soldier, Ye Syan went to the palace carrying the magic fishbones with her.

At first sight, the Tuo Huan king was taken with her lovely face and the grace with which she moved in her dainty slippers. He listened courteously while she recounted the story of her golden fish and its cruel end at the hands of her stepmother. Spreading out her fishbones before him, she told of their magic power to grant her wishes.

Unbelieving, the king requested that she demonstrate their power by making a wish for a gold bracelet. In less than a breath, a band of purest gold lay on the table before him. Still unsure, the king asked Ye Syan to wish for a gold ring. In a twinkling, on his third finger appeared a ring encrusted with glittering rubies. The king was jubilant.

"I shall take Ye Syan for my wife, and she will be forever at my side," he announced to his courtiers.

From the day of their marriage, the temptation of the magic fishbones gave the Tuo Huan king no peace. He demanded that Ye Syan ask them for more and more precious gifts to fill the coffers of his island kingdom. Although his wealth increased a hundred-fold, his thirst for still greater riches was never slaked.

After a time the bones grew weary of satisfying the

greedy ruler's incessant requests. They would give no more. Disgusted with their lack of response, the king ordered Ye Syan to discard them.

But Ye Syan remembered the golden carp that had befriended her in her loneliest and most desperate hours. She gently placed the bones in a silken pouch and carried them a great distance to a remote spot on the beach. With her own hands she dug a bowl-shaped hole. Wishing each bone a fond farewell, she lowered them into the cool earth. Reverently she marked their burying place with a circle of precious pearls.

The waves that lapped the shore flowed endlessly in and out. The tide rose and ebbed. The water scoured the beach and carried the bones out to sea.

SECRETLY

Secretly I loved the giants
fee-fo-fuming their way
through fairy tales—great
bumblers they were, falling
down beanstalks, never quite
right in the head, never a match
for the gutsy tailor or the boy
with a slingshot.

Consider the giant—
put yourself in his place.

You're tall as a house,
can't take a step without
flattening a field, toppling
a barn. Who can you talk to?
Never a voice—just roars
and grunts of the giants
you battle. No conversation,
no style.

By the end of the day
it's comfort you want, a good fire,
bags of silver to count.
What you need is a snooze
after dinner, your harp
to play you to sleep.
Ah harp that sings of Time
before time, songs of your race,
the Titans.

You dream that nothing can touch
this room, this castle.
When a visitor comes, all sweaty
with climbing, he's too stringy
to eat, too stupid to talk to.
The beanstalk shakes with your rage
and you can't fall asleep
for hours.

RUTH ROSTON

The Graveyard Wager

An urban legend
retold by Jan Harold Brunvand

Here's another old horror legend remembered by a reader. This one was sent to me by Vonnie Shepherd of Bloomington, Indiana, who writes, "I grew up hearing this story in a small town in central Kentucky:

"Several girls were sleeping over at one girl's home while the parents were away. After the lights were out, they started talking about the recent burial of an old man in the nearby cemetery. A rumor was going around that the man had been buried alive and had been heard trying to claw his way out.

"One girl laughed at the idea, so they dared her to go out and visit the grave. As proof that she had gone, she was to drive a stake into the earth above the grave.

"They sent their friend off on her errand and shut off the lights again, expecting her to return right away.

"But an hour passed, and then another, without any sign of the girl. The others lay awake, gradually growing terrified. Morning came, and she still hadn't returned.

"Later that day, the girl's parents arrived home, and parents and friends went together to the cemetery.

"They found the girl lying on the grave—dead. When she squatted down to push the wooden stake into the ground, she drove it through the hem of her skirt. When she tried to stand up and couldn't, she thought the dead man had grabbed hold of her—and she died instantly of fright."

This is a nicely modernized version of a narrative that is so old and widespread that we folklorists even have a number for it.

In *The Types of the Folktale*, a standard index of folk-narrative plots, the story is listed as "Type 1676B, Clothing Caught in Graveyard." Usually, though, we folklorists just call it "The Graveyard Wager."

Variations on the basic theme have been recorded since the Middle Ages in Europe and have migrated to much of the world. It's one of those stories that no one really believes—would anyone actually die "of fright"? But the story keeps going around, nevertheless.

In some versions, a soldier bets that he has the courage to remain overnight in a cemetery, but he dies from fright after plunging his sword through his long cloak. In others, a drunken man drives his dagger through the hem of his overcoat. Sometimes the person visiting the grave is told to drive a nail into a wooden cross, and the nail goes through part of his garment.

In a few versions the graveyard visitor suffers just a good scare and a cold night in the cemetery, rather than death.

Vonnie Shepherd's version updates the story so it depicts girls at a sleepover party. It is convincing: a rumor about a man buried alive is the kind of thing teen-agers will talk about once the lights are out.

The references to a person buried alive and a stake plunged into a grave, though, make it sound as if these girls have been reading too much Edgar Allen Poe or watching vampire films.

A more elaborate update of "The Graveyard Wager" story was sent to me recently by G. L. Maclean, a professor at the University of Natal, Republic of South Africa. He says he first heard it twenty or thirty years ago, when university students there were still required to wear academic gowns at their evening meals.

"One evening at dinner," Professor Maclean wrote, "three medical students at the University of Cape Town were talking about a body they had seen lying on the mortuary slab at the hospital adjacent to the medical school.

"They dared each other to take a knife, sneak into the mortuary in the dark, and plunge the knife into the corpse. One student accepted the dare, and the others waited outside while he went in.

"A few minutes after he entered the mortuary, they heard a scream, and fled in terror.

"The next morning their colleague was found lying dead on the floor, the knife firmly plunged into the corpse, and also through the long sleeve of his black academic gown. The fright of thinking he was being pulled back by the corpse caused him to die of a heart attack."

Professor Maclean suggests that by substituting a white lab coat for the academic gown, the story might fit medical students anywhere in the world.

Although I have never encountered such a form of "The Graveyard Wager," I won't be surprised if I do. This traditional story has successfully made the leap into urban legendhood.

The Fork in the Graveyard

A legend retold by Julie V. Watson

The tale of Peter MacIntyre is as exciting a story of the supernatural as one is likely to find and, as such, is still repeated by the people of Tracadie who puzzle over the episode to this day.

The spirit, or ghost, of a dead man is said to have committed the dastardly deed of murdering our Peter, a Scottish settler, who arrived in the area on the good ship *Alexander* in 1773.

The scene is set [with] men relaxing around the warmth of a stove, chatting of mysterious events. When Peter arrived, room was made for him in the warmth, and conversation continued until one Ben Peters mentioned having seen a light in the old French burying place at Scotch Fort. He described a huge ball of fire, dancing across the graves, and lighting up the whole cemetery.

Peter, the newcomer, scoffed at the idea, boasting that such exaggerations would not keep him from walking through any churchyard, even the Scotch Fort one, on that very night.

There were, he claimed, more devils to fear among his mortal companions than in the resting place of the dead.

His boasting, of course, was quickly taken up on, and the challenge thrown out to do more than brag by the comfort of the fire.

"It's all very well to put on a brave front when yer in the company of humans," piped a fellow lounger. "But going to a graveyard that's haunted in the dead of night, and alone, is a horse of another colour. Why, man, you must be clear off your beam to even suggest such a thing let alone go through with it. That old cemetery may be full of dead men's bones, but it's also full of dead men's spirits."

Peter took offense at the remarks, shrugging off superstitious talk as nonsense. The ire was up in his companions who were slighted by his attitude and quickly a bet was made that Peter should go to the old cemetery and plant a hay-fork in a grave, to prove he had been there. Should he succeed a pound of tobacco would be his.

Peter accepted the challenge, and with a jaunty air left the cabin, telling them to have his tobacco ready on the morn, for "I don't expect to be detained by the dead," he said, "I've never knowed dead people to harm anyone."

As it was midnight, all filed from the store. Peter in a long black rain slicker was given the hay-fork and bid on his way to Scotch Fort while the others scuttled for the dry warmth of their own beds.

Come dawn, all were seeking Peter who it seemed had disappeared. His cabin was empty and cold, obviously vacant for some time. More ominous his livestock was bleating with hunger. With the realization that Peter was not to be found came fear, fear for the fate of a man brazen enough to risk defying the very spirits of the dead at the witching hour on a night that seemed to portray the very depths of Hell itself.

The men armed themselves, justifying their actions by expressing a concern about bears in the vicinity, and set out to solve the mystery.

The cemetery was a small clearing in the heart of the forest, reached by means of a narrow footpath, permitting not more than two persons to walk abreast. Every now and then the search party stopped to peer through the branches of the trees, their voices never above a whisper. Finally they were out of the woods and staring in amazement at the sight that met their eyes.

The handle of a hay-fork showed plainly above a grave situated right in the centre of the graveyard. A large black object was curled up on the ground beside it.

Cautiously the party pressed forward, and, as they neared the spot the black object began to take shape. A few more steps and they raised their voices in unison, "Peter! Can't you speak to us."

There was no answer save the echo of their own voices. MacIntyre's body lay across the grave, his face turned toward them. It was a face frozen in agony, a haunted, fear-crazed face that made the living tremble and wish they'd never seen it.

A hand reached out and grabbed the dead man's collar. The hand pulled hard on the collar but the body wouldn't come loose.

A second hand reached out and grasped the fork. It had been driven into the grave with a powerful thrust and right through the tail of Peter MacIntyre's long black coat.

The**Orphan**Boy

A Maasai legend
retold by Tololwa M. Mollel

As he had done every night of his life, the old man gazed deep into the heavens. He had spent so much time scanning the night sky that he knew every star it held. He loved the stars as if they were his children. He always felt less lonely when the sky was clear and the stars formed a glowing canopy over the plains.

Tonight, he noticed, one of the stars was missing.

Like a worried father, the old man searched the darkness for his missing star. Just then he heard the sound of footsteps.

Startled, the old man looked down, and there before him stood a boy. "Who are you?" he asked.

"My name is Kileken," replied the boy. "I am an orphan and I've travelled countless miles in search of a home."

The man's eyes shone with excitement. "I am childless and live alone. I would be most happy to have you as a companion. You are welcome to live here as long as you want."

And, forgetting all about the missing star, the old man set to making a bed next to his own for the boy to sleep on.

When he woke up the next morning, many surprises greeted the old man. Waiting for him in his favourite bowl was steaming hot tea, made with lots of milk, just the way he liked it. The cows had been milked. The compound and the cattle pen had been swept clean. But Kileken was nowhere in sight. He had taken the cattle out to pasture.

In the evening when Kileken returned, the old man was waiting. "It takes me forever to do all the morning chores," he said. "How did you do everything in time to take the cattle to pasture by sunrise?"

The boy smiled a mysterious smile. "The day begins at dawn," he replied. "I get my energy from the first light of day." He chuckled. "Besides, I'm much younger than you are!"

The old man was still puzzled, but he decided not to ask any more questions. After all, Kileken had been a great help, and he was good company too. They spent the rest of the evening sitting quietly together out under the stars.

Just before going to bed the boy said, "We're almost out of water. I'll take the donkeys to the spring in the morning."

"Good," the old man replied. "While you do that, I'll look after the cattle."

The boy shook his head. "No, no. I'll fetch the water and take the cattle to pasture. As long as I'm here, I'll do all the work for you."

It was the old man's turn to chuckle. "Look, it takes two whole days to go to the spring and back. And it takes another day just to load the donkeys with water. That's a big job for a boy your size. You can't possibly care for the cattle if you're going to the spring."

Again, Kileken looked mysterious. "If you trust me, I can do it," he said.

By sunrise the next morning, the boy not only had fetched the water, but had done the morning chores as well. The cattle were out grazing by the time the old man woke up.

When Kileken returned in the evening, the old man stared at him in silent wonder. His mind burned with curiosity, but something about the boy stopped him from asking questions.

By and by, the rains fell and the land turned a glistening green. The old man's heart was full of joy. His face became brighter and his step more youthful.

Kileken continued to amaze the old man with his strange deeds. But though he was curious, he asked no questions. In time he regarded Kileken as the son he'd never had.

The rains were followed by drought. The sun hooked its claws into the soil and a flaming sky burned up the grass and dried up the spring. Buzzards darkened the sky, waiting for cattle to die of thirst.

The old man shuddered. He watched the circling birds and murmured, "If it doesn't rain soon, we will be dead."

"No, we won't die," the boy said, with a faraway look in his eyes.

A little sparkle lit the boy's eyes. "It's something I learned from my father. He had a hidden power over the drought and he passed that power on to me. But it will work only as long as it remains my secret and mine alone. He told me never to reveal it."

Suddenly an urge to understand everything came over

the old man. "Please, tell me," he pleaded. "You can trust me. I won't breathe a word of your secret to a soul!"

Kileken shook his head. "A secret known to two is no secret," he said. "I must not tell you and you must never seek to know. For the day you discover my secret will be the end of your good fortune."

The drought worsened. The plains echoed with the groans of dying beasts. But under the boy's care the old man prospered. More calves were born than ever before and there was more milk than even a growing boy could drink.

But as the old man's fortune grew, so did his curiosity. Each day his longing to know the boy's secret sharpened until he thought of nothing else. His face became clouded with worry and he seemed to age more than ever.

Unable to sleep one night, the old man sat by the fire. His shadow glared down at him from the wall of the hut. He watched as Kileken slept peacefully, and for the umpteenth time murmured to himself, "I wish he would tell me. I would give anything to know his secret."

Suddenly a gruff whisper came from the wall. "Why don't you find out?" The old man was speechless as his shadow continued. "You could have found out long ago if only you had used your brains."

Excited, the old man whispered back, "What a fool I've been! Now, why didn't I think of that?" Then his face fell. "But I mustn't know. The boy . . ."

"Forget the boy!" snapped the shadow. "How long will you suffer because of a silly little secret that a silly little child wants to hide from you? Besides, he doesn't need to know. You only have to be careful."

For the rest of the night the old man plotted and planned. He would find out how Kileken worked his wonders. He would. By this time tomorrow, the secret would be his too. The boy would never know. He would be as sly as a jackal!

When Kileken got up in the morning, the old man pretended to be asleep. He lay still on his bed and listened to the boy's movements as he did the morning chores. Then the hut became quiet as Kileken herded the cattle out. The old man crept from his bed and followed at a safe distance.

The boy walked quickly with the cattle moving well ahead of him. When he was a good distance from the compound, he stopped. The old man scrambled for cover just in time. Kileken turned to look in all directions.

Satisfied that no one was about, Kileken climbed a rock and raised his arms. Instantly, the sun dimmed as a powerful glow spread down the boy's arms and through his body.

But from his hiding place the old man watched, and what he saw next took his breath away.

Suddenly, he was in the midst of magnificent waist-high grass, beautiful green woods and cool gushing springs. His cattle were drinking blissfully, their udders loaded with milk. A cry of wonder escaped his lips before the old man could stop it.

Kileken turned and saw him.

For an instant the boy looked into the old man's eyes. Gone was the trust they had shared. In its place was only sorrow.

The old man threw himself to the ground with a cry of despair and covered his face as the boy exploded into a blinding star. As he rose quickly into the air, the sun gradually regained its sparkle and majesty.

The old man stood up. Gone was the waist-high grass. Gone were the green woods and gushing streams. Gone were the fattened cattle with loaded udders.

There was only scrub land now, barren and drought-stricken. Thin, scraggly cows wandered about the parched countryside waiting for the rain that should come soon.

Lonelier than he had ever been in his life, the old man plodded slowly home. Waiting for him there in his favourite bowl was steaming hot, milky tea just as Kileken had made it that very first morning. But the hut was empty.

That evening, a lone star shone down from the west. Unlike other stars, it neither flickered nor twinkled. At dawn, ringed by the first rain clouds, it looked down from the east. The old man watched it in sad recognition. It was the star that had disappeared from the sky so many nights ago.

The night that Kileken came.

The star is the planet Venus. At dawn it appears in the east as the morning star. At nightfall it is the evening star in the west. The Maasai call it Kileken, the orphan boy, who is up at dawn to herd out the cattle after morning chores, and who returns to the compound at nightfall for the evening milking.

THE FOX and the CROW

From a collection of Aesop's fables
retold by Margaret Clark

One day a crow snatched a piece of cheese from an open cottage window and flew up into a tree, where she sat on a branch to eat it. A fox, walking by, saw the crow and at once wanted the cheese for himself.

"O Crow," he said, "how beautiful your feathers are! And what bright eyes you have! Your wings shine like polished ebony, and your head sparkles like a glistening jewel. If your voice is as sweet as your looks are fair, you must be the queen of the birds." The unwary crow believed every word, and, to show how sweet her voice was, she opened her mouth to sing. Out dropped the cheese, which the fox instantly gobbled up.

"You may have a voice," he said to the crow as he went on his way, "but whatever happened to your brains?"

Narcissus

A Greek myth retold by Jay Macpherson

As beautiful as Adonis was the ill-fated Narcissus, who from his childhood was loved by all who saw him but whose pride would let him love no one in return. At last one of those who had hopelessly courted him turned and cursed him, exclaiming: "May he suffer as we have suffered! May he too love in vain!" The avenging goddess Nemesis heard and approved this prayer.

There was nearby a clear pool, with shining silvery waters. No shepherd had ever come there, nor beast nor bird nor falling branch marred its surface: the grass grew fresh and green around it, and the sheltering woods kept it always cool from the midday sun.

Here once came Narcissus, heated and tired from the chase, and lay down by the pool to drink. As he bent over the water, his eyes met the eyes of another young man, gazing up at him from the depth of the pool. Deluded by his reflection, Narcissus fell in love with the beauty that was his own. Without thought of food or rest he lay beside the pool addressing cries and pleas to the image, whose lips moved as he spoke but whose reply he could never catch. Echo came by, the most constant of his disdained lovers. She was a nymph who had once angered Hera, the wife of Zeus, by talking too much, and in consequence was deprived of the use of her tongue for ordinary conversation: all she could do was repeat the last words of others. Seeing Narcissus lying there, she pleaded with him in his own words. "I will die unless you pity me," cried Narcissus to his beloved. "Pity me," cried Echo as vainly to hers. Narcissus never raised his eyes to her at all, though she remained day after day beside him on the bank, pleading as well as she was able. At last she pined away, withering and wasting with unrequited love, till nothing was left of her but her voice, which the traveler still hears calling unexpectedly in woods and waste places.

As for the cruel Narcissus, he fared no better. The face that looked back at him from the water became pale, thin and haggard, till at last poor Echo caught and repeated his last "Farewell!" But when she came with the other nymphs to lament over his body, it was nowhere to be found. Instead, over the pool bent a new flower, white with a yellow center, which they called by his name. From this flower the Furies, the avengers of guilt, twist garlands to bind their hateful brows.

M y   B r o t h e r ' s
Christmas Story

A family story by Marie Anne McLean

Constable McLean had worked the last two Christ-mases and he was feeling bitter because he had been given Christmas duty again this year. Surely by now he had enough seniority to have Christmas off. After all, he had a wife and kids, and they wanted to go home to the farm and the grandparents for the holidays. It was a pretty dead shift anyway, the evening of Christmas Eve. He decided to make one last tour of town before he went home to be on call for the rest of the night.

It was cold and dark in the early evening, with the wind bringing in snow. People had finished their last rush of shopping, and the stores had closed for the holidays. The streets were nearly empty. As he drove past the lighted houses, Constable McLean could see, in the windows, groups of people home for Christmas. There were cars with out-of-province plates parked in front of some houses. That should be us, he thought, parked in Dad's yard.

Out at the edge of town by the Mohawk station, he saw a lean figure by the side of the road. It was a young man dressed in jeans and a short jacket, with his shoulders hunched against the cold and his hand held out. He was hitchhiking. When he saw the police car turn out of the alley, he turned away and began to walk purposefully down the road. The constable pulled the car up beside him and rolled down the window.

"Goin' somewhere?" he inquired.

"I'm catchin' the bus to Swan River," said the young man. "I'm goin' home for Christmas."

"I'm afraid you're too late. You know the last bus left about two hours ago. Do you want me to take you to a phone or a motel? It's gonna get colder and you're not gonna get a ride tonight. I don't think I can leave you here. If you're short of cash, I can let you stay in a cell for the night and you can phone your relatives from the office." The constable eyed the young man. He looked like the type that any policeman would prefer to have leave town as soon as possible. He had long, stringy hair and looked as though he had not been on speaking terms with soap or towel recently. He did not look directly at McLean as the constable spoke to him.

"You'd better give me your name." The constable's voice became more official sounding.

The man gave his name and looked down at his feet. "I'm goin' to see my mom. I thought I'd surprise her. I think I can still get a ride if you don't stop me or somethin'." His voice held a weak hint of defiance.

Constable McLean decided that there was probably a whole story there, but he didn't think it was a happy one. "Look, I'm gonna give you some time to catch a ride. There's a phone booth at the gas station. If you don't get a ride, call the station. The switchboard will call me, and

I'll come and get you. Are you short of cash?"

The man said nothing.

"I can give you a bed for the night. I'm not gonna charge you with vagrancy. Just tell me if you can afford a room or if I need to take you to the office."

The man looked away.

"Okay, it's up to you." McLean rolled up the window and drove away. As he watched the figure of the young man recede in the rearview mirror, he called the Swan River R.C.M.P. They recognized the name immediately.

"Geez, McLean. You probably did his old lady a favor, not sending him home for Christmas. He's a useless piece of crap. Wonder why he decided to come home now? Is it as quiet over there as it is here? Come to think of it, why don't you keep him? That'll be your Christmas present to us." The voice on the radio signed off, laughing.

McLean turned home for the evening.

When he got home, he changed out of his uniform and attempted to relax. He tried to tell his wife, Carol, how lucky they were compared to that boy out on the road, or his mother. The more he talked, the more Carol could see how upset he was, too upset for it just to be because he was in a temper about having to work.

"You know you did all you could. If he doesn't get a ride, he'll call. He won't freeze. Quit being such a misery about it." Carol wished he could leave the job at work.

The constable laughed. "Maybe I'm bein' tested. You know, maybe God's testin' me." His eyebrows went up and he grinned to show he was kidding. But his voice sounded almost serious. "I think I'm gonna call up the boys in Swan River. They already told me that they don't have much to do. If they meet me at the border, I could deliver him and he'd be home for Christmas. Besides that, then he won't be hangin' around here making more work for us. I know he won't have caught a ride yet. It'll only take me two or three hours and I'll be back."

He got back into his uniform and set out again. The Swan River detachment only took a little persuading to agree to the plan. They vowed that it was "only because it was so slow," so that no one could construe their motives as having anything to do with Christmas or good will.

The young man was not hard to find. He had stubbornly progressed a few hundred yards down the road. When he heard the plan, he showed his blackened teeth in a weak grin. He climbed into the warm front seat of the car. "First time I got into the front seat of one of these," he remarked.

The trip to the border passed without much speech between the uneasy occupants of the car.

Constable McLean dropped his passenger off into the care of the Swan River members and headed back home. He decided to take the road through the Provincial Park going home. It would be pretty empty at this time of the night, but it would make the trip home shorter by at least a half hour. The wind had increased and he reflected that the road might be icy, but he knew the road well and was not particularly worried.

The idea of home seemed good right now. Near the middle of the park where the trees crowded the road, the deep shadows and icy patches forced him to slow the car. He wondered at the wisdom of his choice. What he met around the next corner made him forget completely about the road, the night, and his discontent.

A family were stumbling out of the woods: a man, a woman, and a child about ten years old. The constable halted the car and stepped out into the cold darkness. They seemed nearly frozen.

They had been cross-country skiing, the man said,

and they had lost their way at twilight. They had feared that no one would be on the road at this time and on this night.

They were shivering with cold and relief as they huddled in the back seat of the squad car. The constable offered them coffee from the thermos that Carol had given him as he left. In a few minutes their story came out. As he drove them back to their rented cottage, he listened and wondered at the circumstances that had brought them here.

They were Russian immigrants. They had scrimped and filled in forms and waited for years to get the necessary permits to move to Canada. They had come here to have a place to raise their family in some kind of economic security. They lived in Regina, where they had found work and a home. They had adapted well to this strange new country, but sometimes they could not bear the prairie any longer.

When Christmas came, the longing for forest became too great and they would look for a place with trees to visit for a few days. About two or three years ago they had discovered the Provincial Park, and now each year they rented a cottage for the Christmas holiday. That was how they came to be here on Christmas Eve.

As the constable took them back to their car, he listened to their story and thought about the way he had been feeling earlier in the evening. They still longed for Russia, but they were determined to make a place for themselves here. Perhaps his life wasn't as difficult as he had thought.

The man reminisced about the days of his childhood. He spoke of going to church with his grandmother on Christmas Eve. It was a custom he had outgrown many years ago.

At last the police car pulled into the cottage's yard. As they got out, they all said thank-you to Constable McLean. They seemed reluctant to break off this moment. The man smiled and shook his head.

"You know," he said, "sometimes I think of those Christmas Eves in church with my grandmother and I think I would like to go again. But I don't. Tonight I think I will go back. Tonight I think I understand why she would take me there."

He looked at his wife and child and then he turned back to the policeman. "I would like to give you something to thank you."

"No, that's okay. I'm glad I was here. You guys be careful the next . . ." The constable began his usual public servant speech, and then he looked in the man's eyes. Something had happened that was important. This man wanted to give a gift in return.

"Well, come to think of it. You guys have this great goalie called Mishkin. If you ever happen to write to a hockey fan over there I'd love an autographed picture." He laughed because this was a strange request.

The man laughed too, but his laughter was a great shout, a shout of joy. "Oh, my cousin! He is cousin to me!" In his delight his accent thickened and his English became broken. "I get it for you. Oh yes." He slapped his leg in his excitement as he stepped away from the car to allow the constable to leave.

Constable McLean drove home silently.

As he sat at his kitchen table afterward, he tried to tell Carol what had happened. The words were not there. He needed no words. He was not thinking of the photo of Mishkin. He was thinking that he had already received the gift.

The Twenty-Six Malignant Gates

A mother's fable from the novel
The Joy Luck Club by Amy Tan

"Do not ride your bicycle around the corner," the mother had told the daughter when she was seven.

"Why not?" protested the girl.

"Because then I cannot see you and you will fall down and cry and I will not hear you."

"How do you know I'll fall?" whined the girl.

"It is in a book, *The Twenty-Six Malignant Gates*, all the bad things that can happen to you outside the protection of this house."

"I don't believe you. Let me see the book."

"It is written in Chinese. You cannot understand it. That is why you must listen to me."

"What are they, then?" the girl demanded. "Tell me the twenty-six bad things."

But the mother sat knitting in silence.

"What twenty-six!" shouted the girl.

The mother still did not answer her.

"You can't tell me because you don't know! You don't know anything!" And the girl ran outside, jumped on her bicycle, and in her hurry to get away, she fell before she even reached the corner.

BLUEFLAG

So that I would not pick the blueflag
in the midst of the pond
(and get my clothes wet)
my mother told me that it was poison.

I watched this beautiful, frightening flower
growing up from the water
from its green reeds,
washed blue, sunveined,
and wanted it more
than all the flowers I was allowed to pick,
wild roses, pink and smooth as soap,
or the milk-thin daisies
with butterblob centres.

I noticed that the midges
that covered the surface of the water
were not poisoned by the blueflag,
but I thought they must have
a different kind of life from mine.

Even now, if I pick one,
fear comes over me, a trembling.
I half expect to be struck dead
by the flower's magic

a potency seeping
from its dangerous blue skin
its veined centre.

ELIZABETH BREWSTER

The Wife's Story

A horror story by Ursula K. Le Guin

He was a good husband, a good father, I don't understand it. I don't believe in it. I don't believe that it happened. I saw it happen but it isn't true. It can't be. He was always gentle. If you'd have seen him playing with the children, anybody who saw him with the children would have known that there wasn't any bad in him, not one mean bone. When I first met him he was still living with his mother over near Spring Lake, and I used to see them together, the mother and the sons, and think that any young fellow that was that nice with his family must be one worth knowing. Then one time when I was walking in the woods I met him by himself coming back from a hunting trip. He hadn't got any game at all, not so much as a field mouse, but he wasn't cast down about it. He was just larking along enjoying the morning air. That's one of the things I first loved about him. He didn't take things hard, he didn't grouch and whine when things didn't go his way. So we got to talking that day. And I guess things moved right along after that, because pretty soon he was over here pretty near all the time. And my sister said—see, my parents had moved out the year before and gone South, leaving us the place—my sister said, kind of teasing but serious, "Well! If he's going to be here every day and half the night, I guess there isn't room for me!" And she moved out—just down the way. We've always been real close, her and me. That's the sort of thing doesn't ever change. I couldn't ever have got through this bad time without my sis.

Well, so he came to live here. And all I can say is, it was the happy year of my life. He was just purely good to me. A hard worker and never lazy, and so big and fine-looking. Everybody looked up to him, you know, young as he was. Lodge Meeting nights, more and more often they had him to lead the singing. He had such a beautiful voice, and he'd lead off strong, and the others following and joining in, high voices and low. It brings the shivers on me now to think of it, hearing it, nights when I'd stayed home from meeting when the children was babies—the singing coming up through the trees there, and the moonlight, summer nights, the full moon shining. I'll never hear anything so beautiful. I'll never know a joy like that again.

It was the moon, that's what they say. It's the moon's fault, and the blood. It was in his father's blood. I never knew his father, and now I wonder what become of him. He was from up Whitewater way, and had no kin around here. I always thought he went back there, but now I don't know. There was some talk about him, tales, that come out after what happened to my husband. It's some-thing runs in the blood, they say, and it may never come out, but if it does, it's the change of the moon that does it.

Always it happens in the dark of the moon. When every-body's home asleep. Something comes over the one that's got the curse in his blood, they say, and he gets up because he can't sleep, and goes out into the glaring sun, and goes off all alone—drawn to find those like him. And it may be so, because my husband would do that. I'd half rouse and say, "Where you going to?" and he'd say, "Oh, hunting, be back this evening," and it wasn't like him, even his voice was different. But I'd be so sleepy, and not wanting to wake the kids, and he was so good and responsible, it was no call of mine to go asking "Why?" and "Where?" and all like that.

So it happened that way maybe three times or four. He'd come back late, and worn out, and pretty near cross for one so sweet-tempered—not wanting to talk about it. I figured everybody got to bust out now and then, and nagging never helped anything. But it did begin to worry me. Not so much that he went, but that he come back so tired and strange. Even, he smelled strange. It made my hair stand up on end. I could not endure it and I said, "What is that—those smells on you? All over you!" And he said, "I don't know," real short, and made like he was sleeping. But he went down when he thought I wasn't noticing, and washed and washed himself. But those smells stayed in his hair, and in our bed, for days.

And then the awful thing. I don't find it easy to tell about this. I want to cry when I have to bring it to my mind. Our youngest, the little one, my baby, she turned from her father. Just overnight. He come in and she got scared-looking stiff, with her eyes wide, and then she begun to cry and try to hide behind me. She didn't yet talk plain but she was saying over and over, "Make it go away! Make it go away!"

The look in his eyes, just for one moment, when he

heard that. That's what I don't want ever to remember. That's what I can't forget. The look in his eyes looking at his own child.

I said to the child, "Shame on you, what's got into you?"—scolding, but keeping her right up close to me at the same time, because I was frightened too. Frightened to shaking.

He looked away then and said something like, "Guess she just waked up dreaming," and passed it off that way. Or tried to. And so did I. And I got real mad with my baby when she kept on acting crazy scared of her own dad. But she couldn't help it and I couldn't change it.

He kept away that whole day. Because he knew, I guess. It was just beginning dark of the moon.

It was hot and close inside, and dark, and we'd all been asleep some while, when something woke me up. He wasn't there beside me. I heard a little stir in the passage, when I listened. So I got up, because I could bear it no longer. I went out into the passage, and it was light there, hard sunlight coming in from the door. And I saw him standing just outside, in the tall grass by the entrance. His head was hanging. Presently he sat down, like he felt weary, and looked down at his feet. I held still, inside, and watched—I didn't know what for.

And I saw what he saw. I saw the changing. In his feet, it was, first. They got long, each foot got longer, stretching out, the toes stretching out and the foot getting long, and fleshy, and white. And no hair on them.

The hair begun to come away all over his body. It was like his hair fried away in the sunlight and was gone. He was white all over, then, like a worm's skin. And he turned his face. It was changing while I looked. It got flatter and flatter, the mouth flat and wide, and the teeth grinning flat and dull, and the nose just a knob of flesh with nostril holes, and the ears gone, and the eyes gone blue—blue, with white rims around the blue—staring at me out of that flat, soft, white face.

He stood up then on two legs.

I saw him, I had to see him, my own dear love, turned into the hateful one.

I couldn't move, but as I crouched there in the passage staring out into the day I was trembling and shaking with a growl that burst out into a crazy, awful howling. A grief howl and a terror howl and a calling howl. And the others heard it, even sleeping, and woke up.

It stared and peered, that thing my husband had turned into, and shoved its face up to the entrance of our house. I was still bound by mortal fear, but behind me the children had waked up, and the baby was whimpering. The mother anger come into me then, and I snarled and crept forward.

The man thing looked around. It had no gun, like the ones from the man places do. But it picked up a heavy fallen tree-branch in its long white foot, and shoved the end of that down into our house, at me. I snapped the end of it in my teeth and started to force my way out, because I knew the man would kill our children if it could. But my sister was already coming. I saw her running at the man with her head low and her mane high and her eyes yellow as the winter sun. It turned on her and raised up that branch to hit her. But I come out of the doorway, mad with the mother anger, and the others all were coming, answering my call, the whole pack gathering, there in that blind glare and heat of the sun at noon.

The man looked round at us and yelled out loud, and brandished the branch it held. Then it broke and ran, heading for the cleared fields and plowlands, down the mountainside. It ran, on two legs, leaping and weaving, and we followed it.

I was last, because love still bound the anger and the fear in me. I was running when I saw them pull it down. My sister's teeth were in its throat. I got there and it was dead. The others were drawing back from the kill, because of the taste of the blood, and the smell. The younger ones were cowering and some crying, and my sister rubbed her mouth against her forelegs over and over to get rid of the taste. I went up close because I thought if the thing was dead the spell, the curse must be done, and my husband could come back—alive, or even dead, if I could only see him, my true love, in his true form, beautiful. But only the dead man lay there white and bloody. We drew back and back from it, and turned and ran, back up into the hills, back to the woods of the shadows and the twilight and the blessed dark.

The Dinner Party

A short story by Mona Gardner

The country is India. A colonial official and his wife are giving a large dinner party. They are seated with their guests—army officers and government attachés and their wives, and a visiting American naturalist—in their spacious dining room, which has a bare marble floor, open rafters, and wide glass doors opening onto a veranda.

A spirited discussion springs up between a young girl who insists that women have outgrown the jumping-on-a-chair-at-the-sight-of-a-mouse era and a colonel who says that they haven't.

"A woman's unfailing reaction in any crisis," the colonel says, "is to scream. And while a man may feel like it, he has that ounce more of nerve control than a woman has. And that last ounce is what counts."

The American does not join in the argument but watches the other guests. As he looks, he sees a strange expression come over the face of the hostess. She is staring straight ahead, her muscles contracting slightly. With a slight gesture she summons the servant standing behind her chair and whispers to him. The servant's eyes widen, and he quickly leaves the room.

Of the guests, none except the American notices this or sees the servant place a bowl of milk on the veranda just outside the open doors.

The American comes to with a start. In India, milk in a bowl means only one thing—bait for a snake. He realizes there must be a cobra in the room. He looks up at the rafters—the likeliest place—but they are bare. Three corners of the room are empty, and in the fourth the servants are waiting to serve the next course. There is only one place left—under the table.

His first impulse is to jump back and warn the others, but he knows the commotion would frighten the cobra into striking. He speaks quickly, the tone of his voice so arresting that it sobers everyone.

"I want to know just what control everyone at this table has. I will count three hundred—that's five minutes—and not one of you is to move a muscle. Those who move will forfeit fifty rupees. Ready!"

The twenty people sit like stone images while he counts. He is saying ". . . two hundred and eighty . . ." when, out of the corner of his eye, he sees the cobra emerge and make for the bowl of milk. Screams ring out as he jumps to slam the veranda doors safely shut.

"You were right, Colonel!" the host exclaims. "A man has just shown us an example of perfect control."

"Just a minute," the American says, turning to his hostess. "Mrs. Wynnes, how did you know that cobra was in the room?"

A faint smile lights up the woman's face as she replies: "Because it was crawling across my foot."

THE STORY-TELLER

A short story by Saki

It was a hot afternoon, and the railway carriage was correspondingly sultry, and the next stop was at Templecombe, nearly an hour ahead. The occupants of the carriage were a small girl, and a smaller girl, and a small boy. An aunt belonging to the children occupied one corner seat, and the further corner seat on the opposite side was occupied by a bachelor who was a stranger to their party, but the small girls and the small boy emphatically occupied the compartment. Both the aunt and the children were conversational in a limited, persistent way, reminding one of the attentions of a housefly that refused to be discouraged. Most of the aunt's remarks seemed to begin with "Don't," and nearly all of the children's remarks began with "Why?" The bachelor said nothing out loud.

"Don't, Cyril, don't," exclaimed the aunt, as the small boy began smacking the cushions of the seat, producing a cloud of dust at each blow.

"Come and look out of the window," she added.

The child moved reluctantly to the window. "Why are those sheep being driven out of that field?" he asked.

"I expect they are being driven to another field where there is more grass," said the aunt weakly.

"But there is lots of grass in that field," protested the boy; "there's nothing else but grass there. Aunt, there's lots of grass in that field."

"Perhaps the grass in the other field is better," suggested the aunt fatuously.

"Why is it better?" came the swift, inevitable question.

"Oh, look at those cows!" exclaimed the aunt. Nearly every field along the line had contained cows or bullocks, but she spoke as though she were drawing attention to a rarity.

"Why is the grass in the other field better?" persisted Cyril.

The frown on the bachelor's face was deepening to a scowl. He was a hard, unsympathetic man, the aunt decided in her mind. She was utterly unable to come to any satisfactory decision about the grass in the other field.

The smaller girl created a diversion by beginning to recite "On the Road to Mandalay." She only knew the first line, but she put her limited knowledge to the fullest possible use. She repeated the line over and over again in a dreamy but resolute and very audible voice; it seemed to the bachelor as though someone had had a bet with her that she could not repeat the line aloud two thousand times without stopping. Whoever it was who had made the wager was likely to lose his bet.

"Come over here and listen to a story," said the aunt, when the bachelor had looked twice at her and once at the communication cord.

The children moved listlessly towards the aunt's end of

the carriage. Evidently her reputation as a story-teller did not rank high in their estimation.

In a low, confidential voice, interrupted at frequent intervals by loud, petulant questions from her listeners, she began an unenterprising and deplorably uninteresting story about a little girl who was good, and made friends with every one on account of her goodness, and was finally saved from a mad bull by a number of rescuers who admired her moral character.

"Wouldn't they have saved her if she hadn't been good?" demanded the bigger of the small girls. It was exactly the question that the bachelor had wanted to ask.

"Well, yes," admitted the aunt lamely, "but I don't think they would have run quite so fast to her help if they had not liked her so much."

"It's the stupidest story I've ever heard," said the bigger of the small girls, with immense conviction.

"I didn't listen after the first bit, it was so stupid," said Cyril.

The smaller girl made no actual comment on the story, but she had long ago recommended a murmured repetition of her favorite line.

"You don't seem to be a success as a story-teller," said the bachelor suddenly from his corner.

The aunt bristled in instant defense at this unexpected attack.

"It's a very difficult thing to tell stories that children can both understand and appreciate," she said stiffly.

"I don't agree with you," said the bachelor.

"Perhaps *you* would like to tell them a story," was the aunt's retort.

"Tell us a story," demanded the bigger of the small girls.

"Once upon a time," began the bachelor, "there was a little girl called Bertha, who was extraordinarily good."

The children's momentarily-aroused interest began at once to flicker; all stories seemed dreadfully alike, no matter who told them.

"She did all that she was told, she was always truthful, she kept her clothes clean, ate milk puddings as though they were jam tarts, learned her lessons perfectly, and was polite in her manners."

"Was she pretty?" asked the bigger of the small girls.

"Not as pretty as any of you," said the bachelor, "but she was horribly good."

There was a wave of reaction in favour of the story; the word horrible in connection with goodness was a novelty that commended itself. It seemed to introduce a ring of truth that was absent from the aunt's tales of infant life.

"She was so good," continued the bachelor, "that she won several medals for goodness, which she always wore, pinned on to her dress. There was a medal for obedience, another medal for punctuality, and a third for good behaviour. They were large medals and they clinked against one another as she walked. No other child in the town where she lived had as many as three medals, so everybody knew that she must be an extra good child."

"Horribly good," quoted Cyril.

"Everybody talked about her goodness, and the Prince of the country got to hear about it, and he said that as she was so very good she might be allowed once a week to walk in his park, which was just outside the town. It was a beautiful park, and no children were ever allowed in it, so it was a great honour for Bertha to be allowed to go there."

"Were there any sheep in the park?" demanded Cyril.

"No," said the bachelor, "there were no sheep."

"Why weren't there any sheep?" came the inevitable question arising out of that answer.

The aunt permitted herself a smile, which might almost have been described as a grin.

"There were no sheep in the park," said the bachelor, "because the Prince's mother had once had a dream that her son would either be killed by a sheep or else by a clock falling on him. For that reason the Prince never kept a sheep in his park or a clock in his palace."

The aunt suppressed a gasp of admiration.

"Was the Prince killed by a sheep or by a clock?" asked Cyril.

"He is still alive, so we can't tell whether the dream will come true," said the bachelor unconcernedly; "anyway, there were no sheep in the park, but there were lots of little pigs running all over the place."

"What colour were they?"

"Black with white faces, white with black spots, black all over, grey with white patches, and some were white all over."

The story-teller paused to let a full idea of the park's treasures sink into the children's imaginations; then he resumed:

"Bertha was rather sorry to find that there were no flowers in the park. She had promised her aunts, with tears in her eyes, that she would not pick any of the kind Prince's flowers, and she had meant to keep her promise, so of course it made her feel silly to find that there were no flowers to pick."

"Why weren't there any flowers?"

"Because the pigs had eaten them all," said the bachelor promptly. "The gardeners had told the Prince that you couldn't have pigs and flowers, so he decided to have pigs and no flowers."

There was a murmur of approval at the excellence of the Prince's decision; so many people would have decided the other way.

"There were lots of other delightful things in the park. There were ponds with gold and blue and green fish in them, and trees with beautiful parrots that said clever things at a moment's notice, and humming birds that hummed all the popular tunes of the day. Bertha walked up and down and enjoyed herself immensely, and thought to herself: 'If I were not so extraordinarily good I should not have been allowed to come into this beautiful park and enjoy all that there is to be seen in it,' and her three medals clinked against one another as she walked and helped to remind her how very good she really was. Just then an enormous wolf came prowling into the park to see if it could catch a fat little pig for its supper."

"What colour was it?" asked the children, amid an immediate quickening of interest.

"Mud-colour all over, with a black tongue and pale grey eyes that gleamed with unspeakable ferocity. The first thing that it saw in the park was Bertha; her pinafore was so spotlessly white and clean that it could be seen from a great distance. Bertha saw the wolf and saw that it was stealing towards her, and she began to wish that she had never been allowed to come into the park. She ran as hard as she could, and the wolf came after her with huge leaps and bounds. She managed to reach a shrubbery of myrtle bushes and she hid herself in one of the thickest of the bushes. The wolf came sniffing among the branches, its black tongue lolling out of its mouth and its pale grey eyes glaring with rage. Bertha was terribly frightened, and thought to herself: 'If I had not been so extraordinarily good I should have been safe in the town at this moment.' However, the scent of the myrtle was so strong that the wolf could not sniff out where Bertha was hiding, and the bushes were so thick that he might have hunted about in them for a long time without catching sight of her, so he thought he might as well go off and catch a little pig instead. Bertha was trembling very much at having the wolf prowling and sniffing so near her, and as she trembled the medal for obedience clinked against the medals for good conduct and punctuality. The wolf was just moving away when he heard the sound of the medals clinking and stopped to listen; they clinked again in a bush quite near him. He dashed into the bush, his pale grey eyes gleaming with ferocity and triumph, and dragged Bertha out and devoured her to the last morsel. All that was left of her were her shoes, bits of clothing, and the three medals for goodness."

"Were any of the little pigs killed?"

"No, they all escaped."

"The story began badly," said the smaller of the small girls, "but it had a beautiful ending."

"It is the most beautiful story that I ever heard," said the bigger of the small girls, with immense decision.

"It is the *only* beautiful story I have ever heard," said Cyril.

A dissentient opinion came from the aunt.

"A most improper story to tell to young children! You have undermined the effect of years of careful teaching."

"At any rate," said the bachelor, collecting his belongings preparatory to leaving the carriage, "I kept them quiet for ten minutes, which was more than you were able to do."

"Unhappy woman!" he observed to himself as he walked down the platform of Templecombe station; "for the next six months or so those children will assail her in public with demands for an improper story!"

THE **BARGAIN**

A short story by Jennifer Currie

"Hello Jaimee, it's nice to see you again. What brings you here this time?" her psychologist asked her.

"Oh my dad sent me because of those dreams again," she replied.

"Have a seat and tell me about it."

"Well, it's the same one as always. You know, the one where I remember my mother being killed. I don't know why, she died when I was four which was twelve years ago. Anyway, it begins on a Saturday afternoon. My father had already left for the airport to go on his business trip. Mom was up on a ladder in the driveway painting the top of the garage door and looking after my best friend Sarah and I who were playing with a basketball in the backyard. Then Sarah threw the ball and it landed in the front seat of the convertible which was parked at the top of the driveway. Sarah was in the car getting it out when the car began to roll. It smashed into the ladder my mom was standing on and she fell off and broke her neck."

Mr. Martin leaned back in his chair and stroked his beard.

"And why do you think you keep having these dreams, Jaimee?" he asked.

"I don't know," she replied, "but I have this really weird feeling that I am supposed to somehow change what happened."

"Oh come now Jaimee, how can you possibly change something that happened over twelve years ago?"

"I don't know. It's just like if I can change the dream, I can change reality."

Mr. Martin then began writing vigorously in his notebook before looking up at her.

"Jaimee, I'd like to schedule weekly sessions with you. Maybe together we can help you sort your problems out. Remember, I'm here to help you. I'm afraid our time's up for today but I will be in touch with your father, all right?"

"Whatever," she mumbled to herself.

Late that night as she gazed out the window at the tall pine tree she had planted with her mother just before she had died, Jaimee fell asleep.

≈

"Hi Mommy! Can Sarah and I play in the backyard?"

"Sure honey, just stay away from the wet paint OK?"

"OK Mommy, I promise."

In her dream she watched as the horrible day that her mother was killed took place once again. But something was different this time, something was wrong. Instead of being herself as a child, she was watching the scene take place from across the street. Her teenage self was watching herself as a child play.

"Hey Sarah, catch the ball!"

"Yay, I caught it!"

Jaimee's eyes filled with tears as she watched the scene before her. The children playing, her young, beautiful mother, the laughter, and the happiness.

"Hey Jaimee, CATCH!"

The ball went flying through the air high over Jaimee's head and into the front seat of the car. Sarah climbed in after it and the car began to roll. Jaimee screamed as the car struck the ladder and her mother fell.

"Mommy! Mommy! Oh Mommy! Please somebody help my Mommy!" The young Jaimee was screaming and crying uncontrollably.

Jaimee sprinted across the street only to find her mother's dead body, covered in blood. Filled with rage, Jaimee turned around and kicked the small tree they had planted until it fell over.

≈

Jaimee sat up boltright and tried to catch her breath. Her hair was damp and beads of sweat were pouring down her face. She glanced down at the clock radio which was blinking the time, 2:12, 2:12, 2:12. It was dark out now and the floodlights were shining in the backyard. Jaimee once again began staring out the window into the yard. There was the same garage where it had happened and the pine tree that . . .

"Oh my God, Dad! Dad!"

"What is it, honey?"

"Where did our tree go?"

"What are you talking about Jaimee? We never had a tree out there."

"Of course we did, it was out there just a few hours ago! You know, the one we planted with Mom."

"Oh yeah, I had forgotten about that tree, but what do you mean it was just out there? It was knocked over a week after we planted it, the day of the accident, and we never bothered to replant it. Remember?"

"No! I was looking at it right before I went to sleep. Right before I dreamt that I kicked . . . Oh my God!"

"It was just a dream Jaimee, it's late and you're tired. Now go on up to bed."

"Yeah, all right Dad."

She could hear her pulse pounding loudly in her ears as she climbed the stairwell. Her mind raced as she went over what had just happened again and again. The tree had been there, she was sure of it, but then she dreamt that she had kicked it over. But she hadn't kicked it over twelve years ago in real life, only in her dream. When she had woken up, the huge pine tree was gone. Dad said it had never been there, but it had. She had changed the past! By altering her dream, she had altered reality. Jaimee drew in a quick sharp breath as she realized what this meant. If this was true then she could also save her mother's life! She quickly crawled into bed and snuggled down under her quilt.

"I'll save you Mom, I'll save you," she whispered.

Closing her eyes she allowed the darkness to surround her.

❧

"Hi Mommy! Can Sarah and I play in the backyard?"

The image was back, same as before. Jaimee watched the scene take place from across the street again, this time not in sadness but in hope and determination.

"Hey Sarah, catch the ball!"

"Yay, I caught it!"

Jaimee started across the street towards the house.

"Hey Jaimee, CATCH!"

The ball went flying into the car and Sarah went in after it. The car began to roll and Jaimee began to spring.

She caught up just as it was halfway down the driveway and beginning to pick up speed. Jumping over the door she slammed on the brake and let out a sigh of relief as the car came to a stop, just inches from the ladder.

"Well, I don't know who you are young lady, but thank you. You might have just saved my life. What is your name?"

"Oh my name's Ja . . . Janet," Jaimee replied carefully. "Um look, I really have to go now though."

"Well OK, but I hope I see you again."

"I can guarantee it," she said with a smile.

✐

Once again Jaimee awoke with her heart racing and drenched in sweat. Suddenly she remembered her dream.

"MOM! MOM! Are you here?" she screamed out from her room.

"What is it, honey? Did you have a bad dream?" her mother asked as she came into her room, her eyes filled with concern.

"Mom, it's really you! You're alive!"

"Well of course I'm alive, sweetheart, I'm right here. Are you OK?"

Jaimee looked up at her mother and began to cry.

"I'm just glad that you're all right," she sobbed. "Where's Dad? He must be so glad to have you back!"

"Jaimee stop that, you know perfectly well where your father is," her mother said angrily.

"Oh of course, he must be in the kitchen having his morning coffee."

Jaimee jumped out of bed and ran downstairs into the deserted kitchen. Moments later her mother entered looking very worried and upset.

"Sit down, honey," her mother said softly, pulling out a chair.

"Where's Dad?" Jaimee asked.

"Jaimee, your father died twelve years ago, you know that!"

"What?" Jaimee blurted out. "How?"

"His plane crashed while he was away on that business trip," her mother replied, taking her hand.

"No, he never went on that business trip. He was called back from the airport because of the accident . . ."

"What accident, Jaimee?"

MILLER'S END

When we moved to Miller's End,
   Every afternoon at four
A thin shadow of a shade
   Quavered through the garden-door.

Dressed in black from top to toe
   And a veil about her head
To us all it seemed as though
   She came walking from the dead.

With a basket on her arm
   Through the hedge-gap she would pass,
Never a mark that we could spy
   On the flagstones or the grass.

When we told the garden-boy
   How we saw the phantom glide,
With a grin his face was bright
   As the pool he stood beside.

"That's no ghost-walk," Billy said,
   "Nor a ghost you fear to stop—
Only old Miss Wickerby
   On a short cut to the shop."

So next day we lay in wait,
   Passed a civil time of day,
Said how pleased we were she came
   Daily down our garden-way.

Suddenly her cheek it paled,
   Turned, as quick, from ice to flame.
"Tell me," spoke Miss Wickerby.
   "Who spoke of me, and my name?"

"Bill the garden-boy"
       She sighed,
   Said, "Of course, you could not know
How he drowned—that very pool—
   A frozen winter—long ago."

CHARLES CAUSLEY

A Mountain Legend

A short story by Jordan Wheeler

The school bus drove into a small summer camp at the base of a towering mountain. Boys and girls between the ages of eight and twelve, who had signed up for the three-day camping trip, poured out of the bus. Following instructions from counsellors, they began hurriedly preparing their camp as the sunset dripped over the rock walls towering above them. For many, it was their first time away from the city, which they could still see far off in the distance. Tents were put up and sleeping bags unrolled before the last of the twilight rays gave way to the darkness of night.

Roasting marshmallows around a large campfire, the young campers listened intently to stories told by the counsellors. Behind the eager campers, the caretaker of the camp sat on the ground, himself listening to the stories.

As the night grew old, the younger children wearily found their way to their tents, so that by midnight only the twelve-year-olds remained around the fire with one counsellor and the caretaker. Their supply of stories seemingly exhausted, they sat in silence watching the glowing embers of the once fiery blaze shrink into red-hot ash.

"The moon is rising," announced the caretaker in a low, even voice.

All eyes looked up to the glow surrounding the jagged peaks of the mountain. The blackness of the rock formed an eerie silhouette against the gently lit sky.

The caretaker's name was McNabb. He had lived close to the mountain all his life and knew many of the stories the mountain had seen. He threw his long, black braided hair over his shoulders, drew the collar of his faded jean jacket up against the crisp mountain air, and spoke.

"There is a legend about this mountain once told by the mountain itself," he said, paused for a moment, then continued. "People claim that long ago it told of a young boy who tried to climb up to an eagle's nest which rested somewhere among the many cliffs. He was from a small camp about a day's journey from here and when he was twelve years old, he thought he was ready to become a warrior. His father disagreed, saying he was too young and too small. But the boy was stubborn and one morning before dawn he sneaked out of his family's teepee and set off on foot toward the mountain. There were no horses in North America in his time. They were brought later by the Europeans.

"It took most of the day for him to reach the mountain. The next morning, he set out to find an eagle and seek a vision from the mighty bird, as that was the first step in becoming a warrior. But as he was climbing up the rock cliffs to a nest, he fell to his death, releasing a terrible cry that echoed from the mountain far out across the land. The legend says the boy's spirit still wanders the mountain today."

A coyote howled in the distance and the campers jumped.

"Is it true?" asked one of the boys, with worry and fear in his voice.

"Some people say so, and they also say you can still hear his scream every once in a while."

All around the dying fire, eyes were straining up at the menacing rock peaks. The caretaker McNabb, however, wasn't looking at the mountain, he was watching one of the young campers. He was an Indian boy, smaller than the others, with short braided hair that fell down his back. The boy was gazing up at the mountain, his curiosity obviously blended with fear. Turning his head, his eyes met those of McNabb. For a fleeting moment, they locked stares, then McNabb relaxed, a knowing expression spreading over his face, while the boy continued to stare at him, wide-eyed and nervous.

There were small discussions around the fire, debating the story's truth before the counsellor told them it was time for sleep. Both tired and excited, they retreated to their tent and crawled into their sleeping bags.

The boy Jason lay in a tent he shared with two other boys, who lay talking in the dark. As Jason waited for the heat of his body to warm his sleeping bag, he thought of that long ago boy. He felt a closeness to him and imagined himself in his place.

"Hey Jason, why don't you climb up that mountain tomorrow morning and try to catch an eagle?" It was Ralph, who was against the far wall of the tent on the other side of Barry.

"Why?" asked Jason.

"You're Indian aren't you? Don't you want to become a warrior?"

True, Jason was Indian, but he knew nothing of becoming a warrior. He had spent all his life in the city.

All he knew of his heritage was what his grandmother told him from time to time, which wasn't much. He had been to three pow wows in his life, all at a large hall not far from his house, but he never learned very much. His time was spent eating hot dogs, drinking pop, and watching the older boys play pool in the adjoining rooms. Little as he knew though, he wanted Ralph and Barry to think he knew a lot.

"No. It's not time for me to be a warrior yet," he told them.

"Why not?" Barry asked.

"It just isn't, that's all," Jason said, not knowing a better answer.

"You're chicken, you couldn't climb that mountain if you tried," Ralph charged.

"I'm not chicken! I could climb that mountain, no problem. It just isn't time yet."

"You're chicken," Ralph said again.

"Go to sleep!" boomed a voice across the campground.

Ralph gave out three chicken clucks and rolled over to sleep.

Jason lay there in mild anger. He hated being called a chicken and if the counsellor hadn't shouted at that moment, he would have given Ralph a swift punch. But Ralph was right, the mountain did scare him.

With his anger subsiding, he drifted into a haunting sleep, filled with dreams. Dreams where the wind swept through the camp, gently spreading the mountain spirit's stories throughout. A coyote's piercing howl echoed down the rocky cliffs, making Jason flinch in his sleep.

The following morning, Ralph, Barry, and Jason were the first ones up. As they emerged from the tent into the chilled morning air, their attention was immediately grasped by the huge rock peaks looming high above.

Ralph's searching eyes spanned the mountain. A light blanket of mist enveloped its lower reaches.

Pointing up he said, "See that ledge up there?" Jason and Barry followed Ralph's arm to a cliff along one of the rock walls just above the tree line. "I bet you can't get to it," he dared Jason.

"I could so," Jason responded.

"Prove it," Ralph said.

Jason was trapped and he knew it. If he said no, he would be admitting he was scared. And there was another challenge in Ralph's voice, unsaid, but Jason heard it. Ralph was daring him to prove himself an Indian. Jason had lived his whole life in a city on cement ground and among concrete mountains where climbing was as easy as walking up stairs or pressing an elevator button. To prove to Ralph and himself that he was Indian, Jason had to climb to that ledge. He knew that mountain climbing could end a life. And there were wild animals he might have to deal with. How was he supposed to react? How would he react? He was afraid. He didn't want to go. But if he didn't?

"What's the matter?" Ralph taunted. "Indian scared?"

At that point, Jason decided he would face the mountain and he would reach that ledge. "Okay," he conceded.

At first, the climbing was easy, but his progress became slow and clumsy as he got higher up. Struggling over uneven ground and through trees, he came across a large flat rock. In need of a rest, he sat down and looked down at the campground he had left right after breakfast an hour ago. He could see bodies scurrying about. If they hadn't noticed by now that he was missing, he thought, no doubt they would soon.

Looking up, he could just see the ledge above the tree line. It wasn't much further, he thought. He could get to it, wave down at the camp to show he had made it, and be back in time for lunch. Raising himself up, he started to climb again, marching through the trees and up the steep slope, over the rough terrain.

A few moments later he heard a loud howl that seemed to come from somewhere above. At first, he thought it was a coyote, but it sounded more like a human. Nervously, he kept going.

In the camp, Ralph and Barry were getting ready to help prepare lunch. McNabb was starting a fire not far away. They, too, heard the howl.

"I never knew coyotes did that during the day," Ralph said to Barry.

Overhearing them, McNabb responded, "That was no coyote."

Half an hour later, Jason stood just above the tree line. The ledge, his goal, was thirty feet above, but what lay ahead was treacherous climbing, nearly straight up the rock wall. He scrutinized the rock face, planned his route and began to pick his way up the last stretch.

The mountain saw the boy encroaching and whispered a warning to the wind sweeping strongly down its face as it remembered a similar event long ago. Jason felt the wind grow stronger, driving high-pitched sound into his ears. Gripping the rock harder, he pulled himself up a bit at a time. The wind seemed to be pushing him back. But he felt something else, too, something urging him on.

When he was about twenty feet up the rock face, with his feet firmly on a small ledge, he chanced a look down between his legs. He could see that if he slipped, he would plummet straight down for that twenty feet and after hitting the rocks below, he would tumble a great distance further. He knew it would spell death and for a split second, he considered going back down. But once again he felt an outside force pushing him to go on. It gave him comfort and courage. His face reddened, his heart pounded, and beads of sweat poured from him as he inched his way higher. Straight above, an eagle flew in great circles, slowly moving closer to Jason and the ledge.

Far down the mountain the search for Jason was well underway, but the counsellors had no way of knowing where he was, as Ralph and Barry hadn't told. McNabb also knew where Jason was, but he, too, remained silent.

An eight-year-old girl in the camp lay quietly in her tent, staring up through the screen window at the sky. The search for Jason had been tiring and she had come back for a rest. She was watching a cloud slowly change shape when a large black bird flew by high above. Out of curiosity, she unzipped the tent door and went outside to get a better look. She watched the bird fly in smaller and smaller circles, getting closer and closer to the mountain. She took her eyes off the bird for a moment to look at the huge rock wall, and there, high above the trees and only a few feet below a ledge, she saw the boy climbing. Right away she knew the boy was in danger. After hesitating for a moment, she ran to tell a counsellor.

Jason paused from climbing, just a few feet below the ledge. He was exhausted and the insides of his hands were raw, the skin having been scraped off by the rough rock. The ledge was so close. He pulled himself up to it, placing his feet inside a crack in the rock for support. Reaching over the edge, he swept one arm along the ledge, found another spot for his feet, hoisted his body up, rolled onto the ledge and got to his feet. There, an arm's length away on the ledge, were two young eagles in a large nest. For several minutes he just remained there looking at the baby eagles. He had never seen an eagle's nest before. He was so interested in the two young eagles he didn't notice the mother eagle circling high overhead, nor did he hear her swoop down towards him and her nest. She landed in front of him, spread her wings, and let out a loud screech. Jason was so terrified, he instinctively jumped and in doing so, lost his balance. Both feet stepped out into air as he grabbed the rock.

His hands clung desperately to the ledge as the sharp rock dug into his skin. He looked down and saw his feet dangling in the air. The wind swung him, making it impossible to get his feet back on the rock where they had been moments earlier. A coyote howled and Jason's terror grew. Again he looked down at the rocks below. Tears began streaming down his face. He didn't want to die. He wished he had never accepted Ralph's dare. He could picture them coming up the mountain, finding his dead body among the rocks, and crying over him. He began crying out loud and heard it echoing off the rock. Or he thought it was an echo. He stopped and listened. There was more crying, but not from him. Again he felt the presence of something or someone else. The wind swirled in and whispered to Jason the mountain's legend.

Though running swiftly, the boy Muskawashee had paced himself expertly for the day's journey. He would arrive at the base of the mountain far earlier than he had expected and would have plenty of daylight left to catch his supper and find a spot for a good night's sleep. Though small and having seen only twelve summers, his young body was strong. He would be able to reach the mountain in only two runs, pausing in between to catch a rabbit for lunch.

As his powerful legs moved him gracefully across the prairie, he thought back to the conversation with his father the day before. He had explained how most of his friends were already in preparation for manhood and he felt he was ready also. He did not want to wait for the next summer.

When some of his friends came back later that day from a successful buffalo hunt, he decided he would go to the mountain alone and seek a vision from the eagle.

He knew he would have to rise before the sun to get out of camp without being seen.

When he reached the base of the mountain, the sun was still well above the horizon. He sat down in a sheltered area for a rest. He decided this was where he would sleep for the night.

After a few minutes, he got up and made himself a trap for a rabbit and planted it. After laying the trap, he wandered off to look for some berries to eat while preparing his mind for the following day when he would climb the mountain. After some time, he returned to his trap and found a rabbit in it. He skinned it with a well-sharpened stone knife he had brought with him, and built a fire to cook his meal. He would keep the fire burning all night to keep away the wild animals while he slept.

Finishing his meal, he thanked the creator for his food and safe journey and prayed for good fortune in his quest for a vision. Then he lay down in the soft moss and fell asleep to the music of the coyote's howls and the whispering wind.

The next morning, he awoke to the sun's warming shine. The still-smouldering fire added an aroma of burnt wood to the fresh air. He again prayed to the creator for good fortune in his quest for a vision and for a safe journey up the mountain. When he finished, he looked up, high above, and saw eagles flying to and from a rock ledge. This would be his goal.

Half an hour later, he stood where the trees stopped growing and the bare rock began. His powerful body had moved steadily through the trees even though he wasn't used to uphill running. Without resting, he continued his climb, knowing he would have to be careful ahead. The mountain could be dangerous and its spirit could be evil.

As he pulled himself up the face of the rock, he heard the mountain spirit warning him to stay away. Its voice was the whispering wind, which grew stronger and seemed to be trying to push him back. With determination, Muskawashee climbed. High above, the powerful eagle circled its nest.

Just five feet below the ledge, Muskawashee paused. He was dripping with perspiration from fighting the wind and the mountain. Though scared, he would not let fear overcome him. His desire for manhood was stronger. His hands were hurting and covered in blood from the climb, but he reached out again. After several scrabbling attempts, he was able to grab hold of the ledge and pull himself up onto the narrow, flat edge. Eye to eye with two baby eagles, he stopped. He felt great pride and relief in having reached his goal and stood there savouring those feelings. He didn't hear the approach of the mother eagle. As she landed on the ledge in front of him, she let out a loud screech and spread her wings wide. Muskawashee was startled, stepped back and lost his footing. A gust of wind shoved him further and he could feel his body in the air as he tried to get a foot back on the rock. He grabbed the edge, but his arms were trembling and he could not pull himself back up. His fingers ached and began slipping from the edge. Knowing he would soon fall, he began whimpering. He looked up, into the eyes of the eagle. One day, he thought to himself, he would be back.

His fingers let go and he fell, releasing a loud, terrifying scream that echoed from the mountain, far out across the land, and down through time.

McNabb and one of the counsellors left the camp

when the eight-year-old girl told them what she had seen. Both experienced hikers and mountain-climbers, they were able to cover the distance in a third of the time it took Jason. When they heard the scream, they quickened their pace. Minutes later, they reached the edge of the tree line and looked up at the ledge.

Jason, who had been hanging there for several minutes, also heard the scream and looked down into the eyes of Muskawashee as he fell. Jason felt the tension in his fingers, but sensed there were greater forces keeping him hanging there, perhaps the mountain itself was hanging on to him. Whatever it was, Jason remained high above McNabb and the counsellor, who were watching from the tree line. The wind died down and the eagle stepped back, making room for him on the ledge. Jason hoisted a foot back onto the ledge and tried again to haul himself onto the shelf.

Suddenly, he saw Muskawashee standing on the ledge, extending a hand down to him. Jason grabbed his hand and Muskawashee pulled. The two boys faced one another, looking into each other's eyes. The descendant gaining pride in being Indian, and the ancestor completing the quest he had begun hundreds of years earlier. A powerful swirl of wind swept Muskawashee away, leaving Jason alone before the eagle's nest. Jason reached down and picked up a feather out of the nest.

Below him stood the counsellor and McNabb. They had witnessed Jason's rescue.

"Who was that other kid up there?" asked the counsellor in disbelief.

McNabb smiled and answered. "Muskawashee. He will wander this mountain no more." Then, unravelling a long line of heavy rope he said, "Come on, let's get Jason down."

History of Unchi

"Grandchild, I am an old woman
but I have nothing to tell about
myself. I will tell a story."

They say
that storytellers such as she
hold no knives of blood
no torch of truth
no song of death;
that when the old woman's bones
are wrapped and gone to dust
the sky won't talk and roar
and suns won't sear the fish beneath the sea.

They even say
that her love of what is past
is a terrible thing.
Hun-he . . .
What do they know
of glorious songs
and children?

ELIZABETH COOK-LYNN

The Writing of *Shiloh*

A non-fiction story
by Phyllis Reynolds Naylor

Most of my books begin years before they are ever written. When the idea is too big to hold in my head any longer, it is transferred to one of 10 three-ring notebooks I keep beside my comfortable chair in the living room.

These notebooks, each with the name of a book-to-be in masking tape on the spine, have pockets into which I place photographs or newspaper clippings, maps, and letters—anything at all that will help me in writing the novel. Whenever I get another idea about plot or characters, theme or mood, I just jot it down on the pages of the notebooks so that, when the excitement about a particular book boils over and I'm ready to begin, I already have pages and pages filled with things I will use in my story.

But *Shiloh* didn't begin that way at all. *Shiloh* began 4 years ago with a visit to some college friends of my husband, Rex, in West Virginia. Rex and I rose early one morning and set off for a walk along Middle Island

Creek. We were already beyond the little community called Friendly and had crossed the bridge into the place known as Shiloh, just beyond the old grist mill and school house, when we noticed something following along over in the grass.

I went to investigate and found a dog that I assumed to be a beagle, though in truth it was a mixed breed of who-knows-what. But it was the saddest looking dog I had ever seen—skinny, ill-kept, hungry, and obviously mistreated. Its tail was wagging hopefully, but every time I put out my hand to touch it, the dog trembled and shook, and crawled away on its belly as though I were about to do it bodily harm.

My heart ached for that beagle, and all during our walk both Rex and I tried to get it to come to us—just for a friendly pat on the head—but it didn't work. When we had gone a mile or two, the sky was clouding up, so we headed back, and each time I turned around, there was the dog on the path behind us following. If we stopped, it stopped. When we moved, it moved.

I don't know why, but just on a hunch, I whistled, and the dog was transformed. It came bounding to me, lickety-split, tail going like a windshield wiper, and kept leaping up to lick my cheek, my chin, pawing my shoulder, my legs. Someone had taught that dog to come when it was called, and *not* to come around when it wasn't wanted.

Now we had a second problem: The dog had obviously accepted our invitation and was following us home. As the consequences of what I had done sunk in, I realized I had nothing to offer the animal. We were going back as guests to our friends' home, a beautiful new house with a self-satisfied cat in it. I didn't know whether this dog was a stray or simply lost, and didn't even consider taking it back to Bethesda because we have *two* cats.

It began to rain, and by the time we trudged up the long driveway to the house on the hill, it was raining in earnest. All three of us were bedraggled, and when our hosts let us in, they closed the door firmly in the face of the beagle. The dog went under a tree and lay with its head on its paws facing the house.

All morning I glanced out the window, and the dog was still there. All afternoon I crept to the door; the dog was there. I couldn't help sharing with Frank and Trudy Madden how upset I was that I had whistled, the dog had come, and now I could offer it nothing. I had called it as though I'd meant something, and I hadn't.

Patiently they explained that this wasn't the only animal let loose in these hills—that people frequently drove up from Sistersville and other places and simply let a pet, no longer wanted, go, believing it could survive on rats and rabbits. Most of them couldn't.

Because I was so upset, however, Frank and my husband put the dog in Frank's car, drove back over the bridge, and began asking at a few of the small homes and trailers along the creek if the dog belonged to anyone there. It didn't. At last Frank put it out beside a house with a bicycle in front, and as they drove away, Rex told me later, they saw the dog running down the road after them, but it never caught up. It was then that my tears came.

We drove back to Maryland in late afternoon, and I thought of nothing but the dog—talked tearfully of nothing but the dog. And at last my husband said, "Well, Phyllis, are you going to have a nervous breakdown or do something about it?"

"Something about it," of course, to a writer means writing. It would be a catharsis for me, of course, but it did nothing to help the dog. I wanted to write a story about a mistreated dog, a frightened dog, and decided that a boy named Marty Preston was going to do the talking. In fact, unlike our situation, Marty was going to know to whom that dog belonged and know who had been doing the kicking and mistreating. And the conflict would be what he should do when the dog ran away and came to him a second time. Through Marty Preston, I would rescue that dog.

Three weeks into the story, I received a letter from our friends in West Virginia. They too took long walks in the mornings, and they had kept an eye out for the beagle. And then, Trudy wrote, one morning this "bundle of joy" came bounding out of the bushes. It must have remembered the scent of Frank and his car, for it leaped up, licking their faces, just as it had licked mine, and followed them home. And then, said Trudy, they "made the mistake" of feeding it, and after that, the dog was theirs. They cleaned it up, took it to the vet, bought it a collar, and named it Clover. And now, she said, it's the happiest dog in West Virginia.

I suppose I could have put my manuscript away right then and said, "Okay, it's settled," and gone on to something else. But now I was caught up in the story. Caught up, too, in my guilt about feeling so responsible for this one abused animal when the Maddens had to face this type of thing often. What had I ever done for homeless strays except rescue two cats from certain death and take them in? When was my last contribution to the Humane Society? I had to finish the book to see what Marty would do—could do—when he finds an animal not his own, suspects it is being abused, and decides at last to hide it away from its legal owner, when the choices he has to make are neither black nor white, and he discovers nothing is as simple as he'd thought.

The book took only 8 weeks to write—the first draft,

that is, which I always write in longhand. The second draft as well. It is only the third or fourth draft that I put on the word processor, and then change and revise and edit and delete until I am satisfied that every paragraph, every sentence, every word is the best I can do.

When the book was finished, accepted, and published, I experienced guilt of a different sort. Out of this dog's experience, I got the satisfaction of writing a book; the Maddens got stuck with the dog. What if it barked all night? What if it got in fights with other dogs and was always going to the vet? What if it killed the Maddens' cat?

But then I remembered the springer spaniel we had when we were growing up, and what the love of a dog can mean—always ready to rejoice with you, to be sad with you, to walk or run or play with you, or just sit quietly by the fire. And I decided that maybe the Maddens were pretty lucky after all.

About two weeks after the Newbery was announced, I received an unsigned valentine. No name, no return address. But when I turned the card over, there was a paw print, and then I knew.

Through that Door

Through that door
Is a garden with a wall,
The red brick crumbling,
The lupins growing tall,
Where the lawn is like a carpet
Spread for you,
And it's all as tranquil
As you never knew.

Through that door
Is the great ocean-sea
Which heaves and rolls
To eternity,
With its islands and promontories
Waiting for you
To explore and discover
In that vastness of blue.

Through that door
Is your secret room
Where the window lets in
The light of the moon,
With its mysteries and magic
Where you can find
Thrills and excitements
of every kind.

Through that door
Are the mountains and the moors
And the rivers and the forests
Of the great outdoors,
All the plains and the ice-caps
And the lakes as blue as sky
For all those creatures
That walk or swim or fly.

Through that door
Is the city of the mind
Where you can imagine
What you'll find.
You can make of that city
What you want it to,
And if you choose to share it,
Then it could come true.

JOHN COTTON

Retelling Rat Island

A retitled excerpt from "Gwen" from the novel *Annie John*
by Jamaica Kincaid

It was a while before I realized that Miss Nelson was calling on me. My turn at last to read what I had written. I got up and started to read, my voice shaky at first, but since the sound of my own voice had always been a calming potion to me, it wasn't long before I was reading in such a way that, except for the chirp of some birds, the hum of bees looking for flowers, the silvery rush-rush of the wind in the trees, the only sound to be heard was my voice as it rose and fell in sentence after sentence. At the end of my reading, I thought I was imagining the upturned faces on which were looks of adoration, but I was not; I thought I was imagining, too, some eyes brimming over with tears, but again I was not. Miss Nelson said that she would like to borrow what I had written to read for herself, and that it would be placed on the shelf with the books that made up our own class library, so that it would be available to any girl who wanted to read it. This is what I had written:

"When I was a small child, my mother and I used to go down to Rat Island on Sundays right after church, so that I could bathe in the sea. It was at a time when I was thought to have weak kidneys and a bath in the sea had been recommended as a strengthening remedy. Rat Island wasn't a place many people went to anyway, but by climbing down some rocks my mother had found a place that nobody seemed to have ever been. Since this bathing in the sea was a medicine and not a picnic, we had to bathe without wearing swimming costumes. My mother was a superior swimmer. When she plunged into the sea-water, it was as if she had always lived there. She would go far out if it was safe to do so, and she could tell just by looking at the way the waves beat if it was safe to do so. She could tell if a shark was nearby, and she had never been stung by a jellyfish. I, on the other hand, could not swim at all. In fact, if I was in water up to my knees I was sure that I was drowning. My mother had tried everything to get me swimming, from using a coaxing method to just throwing me without a word into the water. Nothing worked. The only way I could go into the water was if I was on my mother's back, my arms clasped tightly around her neck, and she would then swim around not too far from the shore. It was only then that I could forget how big the sea was, how far down the bottom could be, and how filled up it was with things that couldn't understand a nice hallo. When we swam around in this way, I would think how much we were like the pictures of sea mammals I had seen, my mother and I, naked in the seawater, my mother sometimes singing to me a song in a French patois I did not yet understand, or sometimes not saying anything at all. I would place my ear against her neck, and it was as if I were listening to a giant shell, for all the sounds around me—the sea, the wind, the birds screeching—would seem as if they came from inside her, the way the sounds of the sea are in a seashell. Afterward, my mother would take me back to the shore, and I would lie there just beyond the farthest reach of a big wave and watch my mother as she swam and dove.

"One day, in the midst of watching my mother swim and dive, I heard a commotion far out at sea. It was three ships going by, and they were filled with people. They must have been celebrating something, for the ships would blow their horns and the people would cheer in response. After they passed out of view, I turned back to look at my mother, but I could not see her. My eyes searched the small area of water where she should have been, but I couldn't find her. I stood up and started to call out her name, but no sound would come out of my throat. A huge black space then opened up in front of me and I fell inside it. I couldn't see what was in front of me and I couldn't hear anything around me. I couldn't think of anything except that my mother was no longer near me. Things went on in this way for I don't know how long. I don't know what, but something drew my eye in one direction. A little bit out of the area in which she usually swam was my mother, just sitting and tracing patterns on a large rock. She wasn't paying any attention to me, for she didn't know that I had missed her. I was glad to see her and started jumping up and down and waving to her. Still she didn't see me, and then I started to cry, for it dawned on me that, with all that water between us and I being unable to swim, my mother could stay there forever and the only way I would be able to wrap my arms around her again was if it pleased her or if I took a boat. I cried until I wore myself out. My tears ran down into my mouth, and it was the first time that I realized tears had a bitter and salty taste. Finally, my mother came ashore. She was, of course, alarmed when she saw my face, for I had let the tears just dry there and they left a stain. When I told her what had happened, she hugged me so close that it was hard to breathe, and she told me that nothing could be farther from the truth—that she would never ever leave me. And though she said it over and over again, and though I felt better, I could not wipe out of my mind the feeling I had had when I couldn't find her.

"The summer just past, I kept having a dream about my mother sitting on the rock. Over and over I would have the dream—only in it my mother never came back, and sometimes my father would join her. When he joined her, they would both sit tracing patterns on the rock, and it must have been amusing, for they would always make each other laugh. At first, I didn't say anything, but when I began to have the dream again and again, I finally told my mother. My mother became instantly distressed; tears came to her eyes, and, taking me in her arms, she told me all the same things she had told me on the day at the sea, and this time the memory of the dark time when I felt I would never see her again did not come back to haunt me."

I didn't exactly tell a lie about the last part. That is just what would have happened in the old days. But actually, the past year saw me launched into young-ladyness, and when I told my mother of my dream—my nightmare, really—I was greeted with a turned back and a warning against eating certain kinds of fruit in an unripe state just before going to bed. I placed the old days' version before my classmates because, I thought, I couldn't bear to show my mother in a bad light before people who hardly knew her. But the real truth was that I couldn't bear to have anyone see how deep in disfavor I was with my mother.

A WRITER'S
BEGINNING

From the memoir *Anonymously Yours*
by Richard Peck

I was born with itchy feet and the certain knowledge
that real life was going on somewhere else.

This is a writer's typical beginning. If we were content
with the life around us and thought we were communi-
cating well with the people we already knew, we wouldn't
have to leave town, hole up, and hurl messages at distant
strangers.

Other people being born in Decatur, Illinois, seemed
to think it was a great enough place to be. Some of them
thought it was the center of the universe, but I didn't buy
that. S. E. Hinton was to write that there are people who
go and people who stay, and I was to read her words a
thousand miles from home.

In nursery rhymes, kings were in their counting houses,
and we went with Alice to Buckingham Palace. I couldn't
see any kings or palaces around Decatur. I believed books
and later the black-and-white drama of movies about New

York and Casablanca. I didn't recognize them as fantasies. I thought they were keys to unlock the world, and I wondered how I'd happened to turn up here, miles from anywhere. There was an irony in that, but it didn't emerge till later. Now I've escaped into the wide world that stories promised.

. . . Before I could read for myself, [my mother] read to me. She wasn't trying to make a published writer out of me. She was trying to make me a successful first grader when I got there, and so she intoxicated me with words and opened the door to the alternative worlds found in books.

I heard my first stories in my mother's voice. A satisfactory substitute for this technique has yet to be devised. We read the true-life sagas of Richard Halliburton, a gentleman-adventurer of the day who taught a lot of geography as he went along. We read the children's supplement of the encyclopedia: Aesop, Grimm, Robert Louis Stevenson, a strangely surreal story by a forgotten author, called "The Day the Dolls Came Alive," which haunts me yet.

It was also the golden age of radio, which reached us in ways that television has never quite managed. "Jack Armstrong, the All-American Boy," "The Green Hornet," "Inner Sanctum," and a show with a perfect title: "Let's Pretend." Radio used words: to create characters, to weave plots, to invite the imagination. I lay in front of a Philco radio listening to Edward R. Murrow broadcasting from London and a weekly drama called "Grand Central Station," about how life is better in New York. I lay there, dreaming of being a writer, of using words, in London and New York.

. . . Aunt Rozella, my mother's younger sister, lived with us for the first fifteen years of my life before she married and had sons of her own. I absorbed the dinner-table conversation of my three adults. They talked from three perspectives on the topics people talk about: work, friends, mild scandal, the neighborhood—all the connections of community. It was mid-western talk with a great deal of subtlety at points. A lot was expressed in a look, a turning over of the hand. Here we didn't brawl in the street or even raise our voices, and dirty laundry was never on the line, though reputations were. It was all bedrock for novels. A novel is gossip trying to pass as art.

Permission

A quote by Gabriel García Márquez

One night [at college] a friend lent me a book of short stories by Franz Kafka. I went back to the pension where I was staying and began to read *The Metamorphosis*. The first line almost knocked me off the bed, I was so surprised. The first line reads, "As Gregor Samsa awoke that morning from uneasy dreams, he found himself transformed in his bed into a gigantic insect. . . ." When I read the line I thought to myself that I didn't know anyone was allowed to write things like that. If I had known, I would have started writing a long time ago. So I immediately started writing short stories.

Don't Wait for the Movie

An essay by Gordon Korman

I remember a conversation with a producer who was working on turning one of my books into a feature film. The more I heard, the more I became convinced that I had better savour the moment when "Based on the Novel by . . ." flashed on the screen, because it was going to be the only thing in the movie even vaguely reminiscent of what I wrote.

I think it finally sank in when the producer said, "Well, you know the scene where Steve—?"

"Wait a second," I interrupted. "Who's Steve?"

How ignorant of me to think that, as the guy who wrote the book, I should actually be able to recognize the hero, especially after they plotted, replotted, unplotted, added, excised, and replaced personnel like Harold Ballard. Can't tell the players without a scorecard.

Then I thought of the junior high school student who might someday be called upon to do a book report on my book. He would plow over to the video store to rent *that* movie, save time, and come up with a report destined to flunk with flying colours. (The character sketch of Steve would lay a particularly large egg.) Every one of us has beaten a deadline by condensing a lot of reading time into a 90-minute movie.

All this is hypothetical, of course, because the proposed movie never got made—which is why I am not dictating this piece over the cellular phone in my Maserati. But it did get me thinking about book versus movie, and what makes a book so special, since it obviously isn't time efficiency.

Lately, teachers have thrown us a curve. Now we have to read the book *and* see the movie, and compare the two. Teachers are very big on comparisons. Here it works. Almost invariably, the book gets the nod.

That's not to say that all the movies are bad. After the books, though, they're just somehow incomplete. The novel always seems to have something more—a greater depth, a different perspective, a more incisive insight and humour. There is something unique to the written word— to that relationship between author and reader—which cannot be reproduced any other way. It's more than just reporting or storytelling. It's *different*.

A reader participates in a novel. In a sense, it is almost a collaboration between him and the writer as, reading, he supplies his own interpretation—the reader's draft. No two are ever alike. You can read the same book as someone else without reading the same book. (For instance, everybody who read *Lord Jim* and liked it read a different book than I did. That may be because I'm a poor "collaborator" with Joseph Conrad.) There is a feeling of accomplishment when you come to the end of a very good book—you have completed a successful collaboration. Don't expect royalties.

This is all coming from someone who was a staunch non-reader in elementary school. . . . What finally hooked me in was humour. When I found books that made me laugh, my sense of the "work" of reading was replaced by something wonderful and totally unfamiliar—a desire to find out what happened next. It was a crucial connection. From then on, I equated reading with enjoying myself, and I was a reader for good.

This may sound like an oversimplification, but beware. Relating reading and enjoyment can't be taught; it has to happen. It's a click. Without that click, no amount of explanation, no pleading, no assurance that this is a "great story," will do any good. In my case, humour produced the desired click. But mystery, suspense, adventure, science-fiction, romance, and nonfiction can do the job too. I tend to stick with the funny stuff as the best bet. Tastes can be very specialized, but just about everybody loves to laugh.

My father used to summarize his reading history with the statement, "I read a book once," which was, unfortunately, not greatly exaggerated. Then, out of parental loyalty, he started reading my work. But when I didn't seem to be churning them out fast enough, he tried other authors, and found that you don't have to be a blood relative to appreciate good writing. Now it's not uncommon to find him with a good book in his hand. Reading helps you develop a facility for language, which in turn helps you to read. A neat circle.

Which Way?

A short story by Karleen Bradford

Lauren glanced at her watch as she wheeled her bike furiously out the driveway. Darn, darn, darn! Late again. It was the third time this week and that meant a detention for sure. And she'd even woken up half an hour earlier. Where did the time go to, anyway?

Feeding and organizing the younger kids because her parents had already left for work, that's where, she thought resentfully. When I get married—if I get married—there'll be no kids. Absolutely no kids.

But I'll probably be late for everything anyway, she admitted ruefully. I just can't seem to get myself organized. Even on my own birthday. Especially on my own birthday!

The first bell rang, startling her out of her thoughts. She was even later than she had supposed. Should she take the shortcut across the vacant lot? It had rained during the night and it would be muddy and slippery, but it was shorter. On the other hand, providing she didn't hit the light when it was red, the usual way along the paved street could be faster. She hesitated for a moment, then made up her mind. With a little bit of luck she'd make it . . .

She took the shortcut.

It was even muddier than she had thought it would be, and rougher. And she wasn't the bike rider her younger brother was, even if she did ride to school every day. She followed the narrow trail through the ragged grass, fighting the bumps doggedly. Chris had shown her how to stand up on the pedals and ride with them, but she couldn't seem to master it. Anyway, she was almost through.

A puddle loomed up in front of her. It looked deep— anything could be in there. At the last moment she jerked the wheel to the right to avoid it, and the bike slithered out from under her. Before she knew what was happening, she was flying through the air and had landed in the mud with a jar that shook her whole body. She lay for a moment, trying to get her breath back, then gingerly sat up and surveyed the damage. The bike was muddy, but all in one piece. So, it seemed, was she.

"Hey. Are you okay?"

The voice seemed to come from somewhere behind her. Still dazed, she turned her head and found herself looking up into what she immediately decided was the nicest face she had ever seen. It had a worried frown on it, but as she found herself smiling involuntarily, it split into a big, lopsided grin.

Mouth decidedly too big, she thought. Ears, too. But cute eyes.

The boy facing her seemed to be a couple of years older than she, and when he leaned down to give her a hand up she realized just how tall he was. Dimly, in the distance, she heard the final bell ring. Somehow or other it didn't seem to matter a bit anymore.

Well, she thought. Happy Birthday to me!

Continued on page 92

She took the long way.

As she turned the corner she saw that the light was red.

Turn green, she ordered it silently. Turn green. Without slowing down she headed for the corner, willing the light to change. Just as she reached it, it did. She put on a burst of speed and flashed out into the intersection. She heard the final bell ring at the same moment she heard the frantic squeal of brakes.

When she woke up she seemed to be in a cage, and bright lights were glaring down into her eyes. She tried to move her head and found that she couldn't. She lifted one arm up to find out what was holding her immobile, and pain shot through her chest. She looked down. Bandages swathed her from waist to neck. Then she remembered the accident.

"Hi," said a cheerful voice beside her.

She swiveled her eyes carefully to the left. A small boy was standing beside her bed with a bandage on his neck. A needle was taped into the back of his left hand, and a tube ran from it up to a bottle that was hanging from a tall, coat-rack sort of thing on wheels.

"This is Roly," the boy said happily. "I have to stay hooked up to him because I threw up for one whole day after my operation. I'm taking him down to the playroom to watch TV."

Lauren tried to nod her head, then winced. She closed her eyes and blinked back the tears she could feel welling up.

A week later she could walk around the ward, but she still had to stay in the hospital under observation for the concussion. Brian, the boy who had introduced her to Roly, had made a speedy recovery from the surgery to remove a benign tumor from his neck, and had already gone home. One child who would not be going home was

Continued on page 93

Lauren sat at the kitchen table, a faint smile on her face, remembering that day so long ago. Her parents had had a fit when she had dropped out of college to marry Brad the day after he graduated and join him in a backpacking trip to the mountains of Nepal. They had had an even bigger fit when she and Brad had chosen to spend the first seven years of their married life "traipsing from country to country," as they put it, working in various aid programs.

A door slammed upstairs and she braced herself for the morning pandemonium.

"Morning, Mom! What's for breakfast?" Ten-year-old Jody burst into the room like a bomb.

"Morning, Mom. Is my blue skirt washed?" Deborah, beginning to get gawky at twelve, was right behind him.

"Have you kids forgotten what day this is?" a deeper voice bellowed from the doorway.

Lauren looked up with a smile. The same lopsided grin, mouth too big and ears, too. But the eyes were still cute. Brad leaned down (way down), and hugged her.

"Happy Birthday," he said more quietly.

She was immediately submerged in children.

"Happy Birthday!" they yelled.

"Of course we hadn't forgotten," Deborah said when she had her dignity back. "Mom, Dad said he'd pick us up at school and we'll meet you on campus. The ceremony's at three-thirty, remember? And, Mom, try not to be late." There was a note of pained resignation in her voice.

"She wouldn't dare be late to her own graduation!" Jody exclaimed.

Her own graduation. Today she'd receive her Master's Degree in Sociology. It had been a long, hard struggle—of course she wouldn't be late. Automatically she began to list all the things she had to do before three-thirty.

With a little bit of luck she'd make it . . .

the little girl who lay in the bed beside her. She lay still and quiet, staring apparently sightlessly at the ceiling. Tubes ran into her mouth, her nose, and out from under the sheet that covered her frail wisp of a body. The first day she had seen her, Lauren had turned away with an involuntary shudder of distaste born of fear.

Why don't they draw the curtains around her? she had thought defensively. But then she watched as her parents took turns visiting her. They sat by her bedside and read stories and talked to her as if she could hear and respond. One day Lauren finally said good morning to her and smiled at her when she woke up, and to her shock saw the child's eyes widen and brighten. From then on she chattered to her as much as she did to the other children in the ward. When the nurses told her there was a place for her now in a semi-private room, she refused. By the end of the week she knew every child in the ward by name and was helping the nurses at mealtimes, feeding any who needed help. When she finally went home she found herself falling into the habit of coming back to visit and play with the children, even after the ones who had been in with her had all left.

She smiled now as she remembered that time, then checked her watch hurriedly. As usual, she was running late. She had two operations scheduled for this morning: a two-year-old with spina-bifida and a baby with a club-foot. Then a bit of lunch, then rounds in the Pediatric Ward—the part of her work she liked best, she sometimes thought—then two hours of consultations at the clinic. It would be a full day.

And she had to be home in time to shower and change and meet a very special friend. After all, it was her birthday.

With a little bit of luck she'd make it . . .

Jeremiah's Song

A short story by Walter Dean Myers

I knowed my cousin Ellie was gonna be mad when
Macon Smith come around to the house. She didn't have
no use for Macon even when things was going right, and
when Grandpa Jeremiah was fixing to die I just knowed
she wasn't gonna be liking him hanging around. Grandpa
Jeremiah raised Ellie after her folks died and they used to
be real close. Then she got to go on to college and when
she come back the first year she was different. She didn't
want to hear all them stories he used to tell her anymore.
Ellie said the stories wasn't true, and that's why she didn't
want to hear them.

I didn't know if they was true or not. Tell the truth I
didn't think much on it either way, but I liked to hear
them stories. Grandpa Jeremiah said they wasn't stories
anyway, they was songs.

"They the songs of my people," he used to say.

I didn't see how they was songs, not regular songs

anyway. Every little thing we did down in Curry seemed to matter to Ellie that first summer she come home from college. You couldn't do nothin' that was gonna please her. She didn't even come to church much. 'Course she come on Sunday or everybody would have had a regular fit, but she didn't come on Thursday nights and she didn't come on Saturday even though she used to sing in the gospel choir.

"I guess they teachin' her somethin' worthwhile up there at Greensboro," Grandpa Jeremiah said to Sister Todd. "I sure don't see what it is, though."

"You ain't never had no book learning, Jeremiah," Sister Todd shot back. She wiped at where a trickle of sweat made a little path through the white dusting powder she put on her chest to keep cool. "Them old ways you got ain't got nothing for these young folks."

"I guess you right," Grandpa Jeremiah said.

He said it but I could see he didn't like it none. He was a big man with a big head and had most all his hair even if it was white. All that summer, instead of sitting on the porch telling stories like he used to when I was real little, he would sit out there by himself while Ellie stayed in the house and watched the television or read a book. Sometimes I would think about asking him to tell me one of them stories he used to tell but they was too scary now that I didn't have nobody to sleep with but myself. I asked Ellie to sleep with me but she wouldn't.

"You're nine years old," she said, sounding real proper. "You're old enough to sleep alone."

I *knew* that. I just wanted her to sleep with me because I liked sleeping with her. Before she went off to college she used to put cocoa butter on her arms and face and it would smell real nice. When she come back from college she put something else on, but that smelled nice too.

It was right after Ellie went back to school that Grandpa Jeremiah had him a stroke and Macon started coming around. I think his mama probably made him come at first, but you could see he liked it. Macon had always been around, sitting over near the stuck window at church or going on the blueberry truck when we went picking down at Mister Gregory's place. For a long time he was just another kid, even though he was older'n me, but then, all of a sudden, he growed something fierce. I used to be up to his shoulder one time and then, before I could turn around good, I was only up to his shirt pocket. He changed too. When he used to just hang around with the other boys and play ball or shoot at birds he would laugh a lot. He didn't laugh so much anymore and I figured he was just about grown. When Grandpa got sick he used to come around and help out with things around the house that was too hard for me to do. I mean, I could have done all the chores, but it would just take me longer.

When the work for the day was finished and the sows fed, Grandpa would kind of ease into one of his stories and Macon, he would sit and listen to them and be real interested. I didn't mind listening to the stories when Grandpa told them to Macon because he would be telling them in the middle of the afternoon and they would be past my mind by the time I had to go to bed.

Macon had an old guitar he used to mess with, too. He wasn't too bad on it, and sometimes Grandpa would tell him to play us a tune. He could play something he called "the Delta Blues" real good, but when Sister Todd or somebody from the church come around he'd play "Precious Lord" or "Just a Closer Walk With Thee."

Grandpa Jeremiah had been feeling poorly from that stroke, and one of his legs got a little drag to it. Just about the time Ellie come from school the next summer he was real sick. He was breathing loud so you could hear it even in the next room and he would stay in bed a lot even when there was something that needed doing or fixing.

"I don't think he's going to make it much longer," Dr. Crawford said. "The only thing I can do is to give him something for the pain."

"Are you sure of your diagnosis?" Ellie asked. She was sitting around the table with Sister Todd, Deacon Turner, and his little skinny yellow wife.

Dr. Crawford looked at Ellie like he was surprised to hear her talking. "Yes, I'm sure," he said. "He had tests a few weeks ago and his condition was bad then."

"How much time he got?" Sister Todd asked.

"Maybe a week or two at best," Dr. Crawford said.

When he said that, Deacon Turner's wife started crying and goin' on and I give her a hard look but she just went on. I was the one who loved Grandpa Jeremiah the most and she didn't hardly even know him so I didn't see why she was crying.

Everybody started tiptoeing around the house after that. They would go in and ask Grandpa Jeremiah if he was comfortable and stuff like that or take him some food or a cold glass of lemonade. Sister Todd come over and stayed with us. Mostly what she did is make supper and do a lot of praying, which was good because I figured that maybe God would do something to make Grandpa Jeremiah well. When she wasn't doing that she was piecing on a fancy quilt she was making for some white people in Wilmington.

Ellie, she went around asking everybody how they felt about Dr. Crawford and then she went into town and asked about the tests and things. Sister Jenkins asked her if she thought she knowed more than Dr. Crawford, and

Ellie rolled her eyes at her, but Sister Jenkins was reading out her Bible and didn't make no notice of it.

Then Macon come over.

He had been away on what he called "a little piece of a job" and hadn't heard how bad off Grandpa Jeremiah was. When he come over he talked to Ellie and she told him what was going on and then he got him a soft drink from the refrigerator and sat out on the porch and before you know it he was crying.

You could look at his face and tell the difference between him sweating and the tears. The sweat was close against his skin and shiny and the tears come down fatter and more sparkly.

Macon sat on the porch, without saying a word, until the sun went down and the crickets started chirping and carrying on. Then he went in to where Grandpa Jeremiah was and stayed in there for a long time.

Sister Todd was saying that Grandpa Jeremiah needed his rest and Ellie went in to see what Macon was doing. Then she come out real mad.

"He got Grandpa telling those old stories again," Ellie said. "I told him Grandpa needed his rest and for him not to be staying all night."

He did leave soon, but bright and early the next morning Macon was back again. This time he brought his guitar with him and he went on in to Grandpa Jeremiah's room. I went in, too.

Grandpa Jeremiah's room smelled terrible. It was all closed up so no drafts could get on him and the whole room was smelled down with disinfect and medicine. Grandpa Jeremiah lay propped up on the bed and he was so gray he looked scary. His hair wasn't combed down and his head on the pillow with his white hair sticking out was enough to send me flying if Macon hadn't been there. He was skinny, too. He looked like his skin got loose on his bones, and when he lifted his arms, it hung down like he was just wearing it instead of it being a part of him.

Macon sat slant-shouldered with his guitar across his lap. He was messin' with the guitar, not making any music, but just going over the strings as Grandpa talked.

"Old Carrie went around out back to where they kept the pigs penned up and she felt a cold wind across her face. . . ." Grandpa Jeremiah was telling the story about how a old woman out-tricked the Devil and got her son back. I had heard the story before, and I knew it was pretty scary. "When she felt the cold breeze she didn't blink nary an eye, but looked straight ahead. . . ."

All the time Grandpa Jeremiah was talking I could see Macon fingering his guitar. I tried to imagine what it would be like if he was actually plucking the strings. I tried to fix my mind on that because I didn't like the way the story went with the old woman wrestling with the Devil.

We sat there for nearly all the afternoon until Ellie and Sister Todd come in and said that supper was ready. Me and Macon went out and ate some collard greens, ham hocks, and rice. Then Macon he went back in and listened to some more of Grandpa's stories until it was time for him to go home. I wasn't about to go in there and listen to no stories at night.

Dr. Crawford come around a few days later and said that Grandpa Jeremiah was doing a little better.

"You think the Good Lord gonna pull him through?" Sister Todd asked.

"I don't tell the Good Lord what He should or should not be doing," Dr. Crawford said, looking over at Sister

Todd and at Ellie. "I just said that *my* patient seems to be doing okay for his condition."

"He been telling Macon all his stories," I said.

"Macon doesn't seem to understand that Grandpa Jeremiah needs his strength," Ellie said. "Now that he's improving, we don't want him to have a setback."

"No use in stopping him from telling his stories," Dr. Crawford said. "If it makes him feel good it's as good as any medicine I can give him."

I saw that this didn't set with Ellie, and when Dr. Crawford had left I asked her why.

"Dr. Crawford means well," she said, "but we have to get away from the kind of life that keeps us in the past."

She didn't say why we should be trying to get away from the stories and I really didn't care too much. All I knew was that when Macon was sitting in the room with Grandpa Jeremiah I wasn't nearly as scared as I used to be when it was just me and Ellie listening. I told that to Macon.

"You getting to be a big man, that's all," he said.

That was true. Me and Macon was getting to be good friends, too. I didn't even mind so much when he started being friends with Ellie later. It seemed kind of natural, almost like Macon was supposed to be there with us instead of just visiting.

Grandpa wasn't getting no better, but he wasn't getting no worse, either.

"You liking Macon now?" I asked Ellie when we got to the middle of July. She was dishing out a plate of smothered chops for him and I hadn't even heard him ask for anything to eat.

"Macon's funny," Ellie said, not answering my question. "He's in there listening to all of those old stories like he's really interested in them. It's almost as if he and

Grandpa Jeremiah are talking about something more than the stories, a secret language."

I didn't think I was supposed to say anything about that to Macon, but once, when Ellie, Sister Todd, and Macon were out on the porch shelling butter beans after Grandpa got tired and was resting, I went into his room and told him what Ellie had said.

"She said that?" Grandpa Jeremiah's face was skinny and old looking but his eyes looked like a baby's, they was so bright.

"Right there in the kitchen is where she said it," I said. "And I don't know what it mean but I was wondering about it."

"I didn't think she had any feeling for them stories," Grandpa Jeremiah said. "If she think we talking secrets, maybe she don't."

"I think she getting a feeling for Macon," I said.

"That's okay, too," Grandpa Jeremiah said. "They both young."

"Yeah, but them stories you be telling, Grandpa, they about old people who lived a long time ago," I said.

"Well, those the folks you got to know about," Grandpa Jeremiah said. "You think on what those folks been through, and what they was feeling, and you add it up with what you been through and what you been feeling, then you got you something."

"What you got Grandpa?"

"You got you a bridge," Grandpa said. "And a meaning. Then when things get so hard you about to break, you can sneak across that bridge and see some folks who went before you and see how they didn't break. Some got bent and some got twisted and a few fell along the way, but they didn't break."

"Am I going to break, Grandpa?"

"You? As strong as you is?" Grandpa Jeremiah pushed himself up on his elbow and give me a look. "No way you going to break, boy. You gonna be strong as they come. One day you gonna tell all them stories I told you to your young'uns and they'll be as strong as you."

"Suppose I ain't got no stories, can I make some up?"

"Sure you can, boy. You make 'em up and twist 'em around. Don't make no mind. Long as you got 'em."

"Is that what Macon is doing?" I asked. "Making up stories to play on his guitar?"

"He'll do with 'em what he see fit, I suppose," Grandpa Jeremiah said. "Can't ask more than that from a man."

It rained the first three days of August. It wasn't a hard rain but it rained anyway. The mailman said it was good for the crops over East but I didn't care about that so I didn't pay him no mind. What I did mind was when it rain like that the field mice come in and get in things like the flour bin and I always got the blame for leaving it open.

When the rain stopped I was pretty glad. Macon come over and sat with Grandpa and had something to eat with us. Sister Todd come over, too.

"How Grandpa doing?" Sister Todd asked. "They been asking about him in the church."

"He's doing all right," Ellie said.

"He's kind of quiet today," Macon said. "He was just talking about how the hogs needed breeding."

"He must have run out of stories to tell," Sister Todd said. "He'll be repeating on himself like my father used to do. That's the way I *hear* old folks get."

Everybody laughed at that because Sister Todd was pretty old, too. Maybe we was all happy because the sun was out after so much rain. When Sister Todd went in to take Grandpa Jeremiah a plate of potato salad with no mayonnaise like he liked it, she told him about how people was asking for him and he told her to tell them he was doing okay and to remember him in their prayers.

Sister Todd came over the next afternoon, too, with some rhubarb pie with cheese on it, which is my favorite pie. When she took a piece into Grandpa Jeremiah's room she come right out again and told Ellie to go fetch the Bible.

It was a hot day when they had the funeral. Mostly everybody was there. The church was hot as anything, even though they had the window open. Some yellow-jacks flew in and buzzed around Sister Todd's niece and then around Deacon Turner's wife and settled right on her hat and stayed there until we all stood and sang "Soon-a Will Be Done."

At the graveyard Macon played "Precious Lord" and I cried hard even though I told myself that I wasn't going to cry the way Ellie and Sister Todd was, but it was such a sad thing when we left and Grandpa Jeremiah was still out to the grave that I couldn't help it.

During the funeral and all, Macon kind of told everybody where to go and where to sit and which of the three cars to ride in. After it was over he come by the house and sat on the front porch and played on his guitar. Ellie was standing leaning against the rail and she was crying but it wasn't a hard crying. It was a soft crying, the kind that last inside of you for a long time.

Macon was playing a tune I hadn't heard before. I thought it might have been what he was working at when Grandpa Jeremiah was telling him those stories and I watched his fingers but I couldn't tell if it was or not. It wasn't nothing special, that tune Macon was playing, maybe halfway between them Delta blues he would do when Sister Todd wasn't around and something you would play at church. It was something different and something the same at the same time. I watched his fingers go over that guitar and figured I could learn that tune one day if I had a mind to.

Lost in the museum

Every glass case in a museum
Is an island surrounded by time.
To reach them you have to imagine
Crossing not seas but centuries
To a different kind of life.

Separated from us not by waves
But all the years that have passed
Are places where they still run
The first steam locomotive
And cheer the speedmen on
In penny farthing bicycle races.

And there with the sickle to cut the corn
And millstones to grind it to flour
Is the kind of shelter we'd build
Were we lost on a distant island
And those are the tools we'd invent
If no one ever came to find us.

STANLEY COOK

Chagall's
Christmas Gift

An autobiographical story
by Isabel Allende

> My uncle said that at night the characters in books
> escaped from the pages and entered the world of the
> living, so I used to lie down in one corner of the bed in
> order to leave room for the adventurers, the courte-
> sans, the pirates, and princesses of the stories who
> came to spend the night with me.

There are significant moments that etch themselves on
the memory, remaining buried in the deepest recesses of
the mind and in the course of a life nourishing the roots
of creativity so that it may bear fruit and flowers. The
scent of honey in summer, the rumble of a storm on the
Pacific coast, a line by Pablo Neruda, a frame from a
Bergman movie, a Dostoevsky character . . . I suppose I've
stored up many such things, which appear in various guises
in my books, though I am aware of very few of them.
There is one, however, that made its mark on me very early

in childhood and whose effect I recall as vividly as if it were yesterday, perhaps because the emotion has repeated itself so many times in my life. It happened the Christmas I discovered Marc Chagall . . . the artist who revealed to me the fabulous possibilities of the imagination.

. . . On Christmas Eve I went to bed in my corner with my legs scrunched up, hoping to wake up surrounded by a mountain of parcels as well as the characters in my uncle's books. On awakening, however, I realized that none of these things were at the foot of the bed; all I found was a box of paints and a pair of brushes, along with a note whose handwriting bore a suspicious resemblance to my mother's. It read as follows: *The walls of your room are yours. You can paint what you want on them.* I looked around and saw that the . . . walls were bare. Pinned to one of them was a colored reproduction torn from an art book. On the verge of bursting into tears of disillusionment, I went over to look at it. It was a painting by Marc Chagall.

At first it seemed to me only anarchic blotches; but I soon discerned in the small torn sheet of paper an amazing universe of red angels and blue goats, . . . and a wan pair of newlyweds rising toward the sky. There were so many colors and different objects that it took quite a while for me to find my way around the marvelous disorder of the composition. This picture had music: the ticking of a clock, the wail of violins, the sound of a bugle, endlessly babbling words, the flutter of wings. It had smells too: the scent of lighted candles, of woodland flowers, of animals. . . . It had real elements, but the whole thing seemed enveloped in the mists of a happy dream. On the one hand the atmosphere was as warm as an afternoon at siesta time; on the other it was as cool as a night in the country. I was much too young to analyze what I had seen, but I remember what I felt: an irrepressible sympathy for every one of those characters, surprise, and curiosity, as if I had found myself in front of an extraordinary conjuring trick. That picture was a never-ending story, an invitation to play.

I stood for a long time examining it, fascinated, and wondering how it was possible to paint that way, without the slightest respect for those norms of composition and perspective that the drawing instructress had tried to teach me at school. I concluded that if this unknown person was allowed to paint this way, I too could create whatever I pleased. I opened the box of paints and attacked the wall. I started by painting a black cat with red eyes and continued with the cars of an interminable train. I spent that day and many more amused by my paintbrushes with a feeling of profound freedom and delight.

Some years later all the walls and part of the ceiling of my room had been covered by a horrendous mural in which I put not only the toys and friends I wished I had but also all my nighttime fears, my temper tantrums, my unanswered questions, my growing pains. In a place of honor, between an impossible piece of vegetation and an outrageous animal, I painted the silhouette of a boy seen from behind, as if he were standing looking at the mural. It was a portrait of Marc Chagall, with whom I had fallen in love as only lonely little girls can.

At the time when I was painting furiously on the walls of a house in Santiago de Chile, the object of my affections, sixty years older than I and world famous, was ending his long widowerhood by marrying Vava Brodsky, and living in the heart of Paris. But distance and time are very fragile conventions. I believed he was a child, like me, and many years later, in April 1985, when Marc

Chagall died at the age of ninety-three, I realized that he was indeed. For me he was always the boy I imagined.

My mother married a diplomat and we began a long peregrination among several countries. I remember the day we left my grandparents' house. Our suitcases were piled in the entrance waiting for the cars that were taking us to the port to catch the boat. The aged maids wept and kissed us and my grandfather, dressed in black from head to foot since the death of my grandmother, occupied himself by giving orders and whacking the ground with his heavy silver cane. I shut myself in my room for the last time and sat on the bed looking at the mural, that strange record of my childhood. My mother came in quietly and sat down beside me.

"It's sad to leave it, isn't it? Everything that's important to you is here, good and bad, reality and dreams," she said.

"Tomorrow they'll come to paint this room and there'll be nothing left of my pictures. Do you think I could make another mural in the country we're going to?"

"Maybe not."

"I have to get it off my chest, mama. If I don't paint everything that's in my head I'll burst."

"Why don't you use a notebook instead of walls?"

"It's not the same."

"No, but it might be better. You could write down everything that comes into your head, everything you imagine, there's no limit to it," said my mother.

And that was the way I had to do it. It was very difficult at first, because the words weren't enough to express what I felt, just little flyspecks on the page, until I asked myself what Marc Chagall would have done in my place, what he would have said if he had been a writer instead of a painter. I decided that he would have colored the words, and applied to my writing the same freedom and joy that he put in his pictures. Since then writing has come naturally to me.

I began earning my living with words at the age of seventeen, working as a journalist, and a quarter of a century passed before I wrote my first novel, *The House of the Spirits*, but I haven't forgotten Chagall's lesson. I'm not a tortured writer; I write for the simple pleasure of it, from the pure desire to tell a story. I've never been paralyzed by anxiety or dread at the sight of a blank sheet of paper; on the contrary, it's always an occasion for celebration. . . . There are several Chagall reproductions in my study; the artist is always close by me to remind me that I must treat my characters kindly; that a good text, like a good picture, does not only tell a story, it also contains smell, taste, texture, light and shade; that reality is a jumble, we can never manage to measure it or sort it out, because everything happens at the same time; that the best way of grasping the world is to dream it. On that long-ago Christmas of my childhood Marc Chagall taught me to be free, and for that I have loved him all my life, with the nostalgic fidelity of first love.

THE REIGATE SQUIRES

A play by Michael and Mollie Hardwick
based on a short story
by Sir A. Conan Doyle

CHARACTERS

SHERLOCK HOLMES

DR. WATSON, Holmes' assistant

COLONEL HAYTER, Former army officer and friend of Dr. Watson

BLAKE, Colonel Hayter's butler

INSPECTOR FORRESTER, A member of the Surrey Constabulary

J. P. CUNNINGHAM, A neighbour of Colonel Hayter

TWO CONSTABLES

ALEC CUNNINGHAM, Son of J. P. Cunningham

WILLIAM KIRWAN, A corpse

SCENE I: The morning room of Colonel Hayter's house
SCENE II: Outside Cunningham's house
SCENE III: Cunningham's parlour

(The morning room of COLONEL HAYTER's *country house near Reigate.* HAYTER *rises as* WATSON *enters. They shake hands.)*

HAYTER. Great pleasure to see you again, Watson, old chap.

WATSON. My dear Hayter, delighted.

HAYTER. Good few years since we were fighting together in Afghanistan, what?

WATSON. Six or seven. I keep forgetting, until the weather turns damp and the old wound reminds me.

HAYTER. Hah! Know what you mean. *(rubbing his hip)* Terrible in a cold snap, isn't it? Still, it would have been a good deal worse without a surgeon like you on hand, Watson. Lucky I got mine before you stopped yours, eh?

(They laugh.)

You've been having an interesting enough time since, by all accounts.

WATSON *(nodding)*. I don't mind admitting, Hayter, I was pretty well on my beam ends after they let me out of hospital. No capital to buy a decent medical practice.

HAYTER. Too bad! Too bad!

WATSON. Then, quite by chance, I met a young chap who said he knew a fellow who wanted someone to go halves in a suite of rooms in Baker Street.

HAYTER. Well, well, well! And that's how you met Sherlock Holmes! Remarkable thing, coincidence!

WATSON. Mind you, I didn't know whether I could stick it at first. If there's an untidier man in London, I'd hate to meet him. Stuff all over the place! Books, papers, chemical experiments going on. Strange people calling at all hours of the day and night . . .

HAYTER. Oh, my word!

WATSON. And what with his fiddle-playing, and his filthy
pipe, and never being there for meals when they're
ready, I reckon he must be about the worst tenant in
London into the bargain. But our Mrs. Hudson wor-
ships him.

HAYTER. Shouldn't be surprised if you do, too, Watson.

WATSON. Well . . . (*He grins, but then looks more
serious.*) But you see what's happened now? Time and
again I've warned him he couldn't go on living like
that. He's never listened to me, and now he's paying
the penalty.

(HAYTER *glances beyond* WATSON *and clears his throat
warningly.*)

HAYTER (*low*). Here he comes.

WATSON. Oh, don't worry about that. I don't mince
words about what I think of his goings-on. At least
this breakdown might bring him to his senses.

(HOLMES *enters. He wears a dressing-gown over his
clothes and his feet are slippered. He is pale and
walks slowly, much pulled-down by illness.*)

HAYTER (*going to him*). Good morning, Mr. Holmes.
Trust you slept well. Breakfast to your taste. Everything. Eh?

HOLMES (*shakes hands with him*). Your arrangements are
admirable, Colonel Hayter. It was . . . most kind of
you to invite me here for a little rest.

(HAYTER *urges him into a chair.* HOLMES *sinks down
thankfully.*)

HAYTER. My pleasure entirely, me dear chap.

HOLMES. I don't mind admitting this has left me feeling a
trifle shaken.

WATSON (*snorts*). Shaken! Complete breakdown, you
mean. (*He turns to* HAYTER.) He'd been working

fifteen hours a day for two months on this Nether-
lands-Sumatra case. He succeeded where the police of
three continents failed. Telegrams of congratulation
pouring in by the bucketful, and then he collapses
completely—and he says he's a bit "shaken"!

HOLMES. Well, it's all a thing of the past for me now.
Springtime in the country and Colonel Hayter's hospi-
tality are what matter for the present.

HAYTER (*laughs*). Let's hope you won't be disturbed by
any more of the fun we've been having here lately.

HOLMES. Fun?

(WATSON, *out of* HOLMES' *sight, makes a warning gesture to* HAYTER.)

HAYTER. Oh! Ah . . . (*Clears his throat.*) Just a bit of nonsense been going on. Nothing at all, what?

HOLMES. You intrigue me, Colonel.

HAYTER. Well . . . dash it, there's nothing to it really. Old
Acton, one of our local squires, had his house broken
into the other day. (*laughs*) Matter of fact, it'll make
you laugh. Never guess what they got away with.
(*telling the items off on his fingers*) Two plated candlesticks, ivory letter-weight, small oak barometer,
ball of twine, and . . . ah, yes—a copy of Homer's
Odyssey.

HOLMES (*sinking back*). Well, the county police ought to
be able to make something of it. Surely, it's obvious
that . . .

WATSON. Now, now, Holmes! You're here for a rest,
remember?

HOLMES (*sighs*). Oh, dear me, Watson. Well, I suppose
I've got to do what *you tell me*, for a change.

HAYTER. That's right, Holmes.

(BLAKE *enters, agitated.*)

BLAKE. Beg pardon, sir.

HAYTER. Yes, Blake? Something the matter?

BLAKE. At the Cunninghams', sir . . .

HAYTER. Eh? Not another burglary?

BLAKE. Murder, sir!

WATSON. Great heavens!

(HOLMES *sits up with interest.*)

HAYTER. By Jove! Who? The old man or his son?

BLAKE. Neither, sir. It was William, the coachman. Shot through the 'eart.

HAYTER. Who shot him?

BLAKE. Oh, it was a burglar, sir. Got clean away. He'd just forced the pantry window open, they say, when William disturbed him. Shot him dead and made off.

HAYTER. When was this, Blake?

BLAKE. Last night, sir. Somewhere about twelve.

HAYTER. Hm! Bad business. All right, Blake.

BLAKE (*going*). Very good, sir.

(*He exits.*)

HAYTER. Poor old Cunningham! Our leading squire about here. He'll be cut up about this, you know. The man had been in his service for years.

WATSON. Might be one of the same chaps who broke into the other place.

HAYTER. I fancy it's someone local, myself. Acton's and Cunningham's are just the places he would go for. Largest in these parts.

HOLMES. And the richest?

HAYER. Well, they ought to be. But they've had a lot of blood sucked out of them in recent years.

WATSON. How's that?

HAYTER. They've had a lawsuit dragging on for no end of time. Old Acton has some claim on half of Cunningham's estate. The lawyers have been at it with both hands.

HOLMES. Well, if it's a local man there shouldn't be much difficulty in running him down.

(BLAKE *enters.*)

BLAKE. Inspector Forrester, sir.

HAYTER (*calling*). Come in, Inspector.

(FORRESTER *enters.* BLAKE *exits.*)

FORRESTER. Good morning, Colonel Hayter. I hope I don't intrude, sir, but we hear that Mr. Holmes of Baker Street is here.

HAYTER (*indicating him*). There he is, Inspector. And this is Dr. Watson.

WATSON. How d'ye do?

(*They shake hands.*)

FORRESTER. Pleased to meet you, gentlemen. You've heard the news, I expect. We, er, wondered if we could ask you to step across, Mr. Holmes?

WATSON. Certainly not, Inspector. Mr. Holmes is recuperating—under *my orders.*

HOLMES (*laughs: brisker now*). Luck is against you, Watson. We were chatting about the matter when you came in, Inspector. Perhaps you'd care to take a seat and let us have a few details?

(WATSON *rolls his eyes hopelessly at* HAYTER, *who grins.*)

FORRESTER. Thank you, sir. (*sitting*) Well, we had no clue in the Acton affair, but we've plenty to go on this time.

HOLMES. Oh?

FORRESTER. The man was seen.

HAYTER. Aha!

FORRESTER. When the alarm broke out, Mr. Cunningham had just got into bed, and Mr. Alec Cunningham—that's his son—was smoking a pipe in the parlour.

They both heard William, the coachman, call for help, and Mr. Alec ran out in his dressing-gown. The back door was open, and he saw the two men wrestling together outside. One of them fired a shot, the other dropped to the ground, and the murderer was off across the garden hedge. Mr. Cunningham saw him, too, from his bedroom window, as he reached the road.

HAYTER. Couldn't young Alec catch him?

FORRESTER. He'd stopped to do what he could for William, so the fellow got clean away. Middle-sized man, dressed in some dark stuff—that's the description we've got.

HOLMES. Did William say anything before he died?

FORRESTER. Not a word. But one thing we did get was this.

(*He fumbles in his waistcoat and produces a fragment of paper.*)

(*holding it up*) Seems to be a fragment of paper torn from a larger sheet. It was between the dead man's finger and thumb.

(*He gives it to* HOLMES, *who examines it keenly.*)

HAYTER. So either the other chap tore the rest of the paper out of William's hand—or William tore this bit from a sheet the other chap was holding. Can't see what either of them was doing waving sheets of paper about.

FORRESTER. If you look at the words, though, it reads as if it's some sort of appointment.

HOLMES (*reading*). " . . . at quarter to twelve . . . " Then down here it says "learn what . . . " Hm! This writing is of extraordinary interest. These are much deeper waters than I'd thought.

FORRESTER. How's that, Mr. Holmes? Do you reckon there was some sort of understanding between

William and the burglar? Do you think William was to let him in, but they had a quarrel instead?

HOLMES. It's not entirely impossible. But this writing . . . (*He peers intently at the paper.*) No . . . (*eagerly*) There's something about it that fascinates me extremely. Colonel, if you'll excuse me I'll leave Watson with you and step round with the Inspector to put one or two little fancies of mine to the test. (HOLMES *almost springs to his feet in his eagerness, handing the paper back to* FORRESTER.)

WATSON. Holmes, you'll do nothing of the sort! I . . . I forbid you.

HOLMES. Never fear, Watson. I feel suddenly better. But I promise to deliver myself up to you in half an hour precisely.

WATSON. Well . . .

HOLMES (*mischievously*). At Mr. Cunningham's door. You too, if you wish, Colonel. (HOLMES *takes* FORRESTER *by the arm and pilots him swiftly from the room.* WATSON *steps forward, raising a hand in protest, but can only turn and shrug helplessly at* HAYTER, *who laughs.*)

HAYTER. Now, me dear chap, I see *exactly* what you mean.

SCENE TWO

(*Outside Cunningham's house. This can be played in front of the curtain.* HOLMES *and* FORRESTER *enter from Stage Right.* HOLMES *is now dressed in tweed coat and deerstalker cap and is puffing his pipe, peering about him intently. From Left two* CONSTABLES *enter, carrying the draped body of* WILLIAM *on a stretcher.* FORRESTER *motions them to put it down. They do so and retreat a few paces to stand respectfully at ease.*)

FORRESTER. Here we are, sir. Sorry you couldn't see it
*in situ**, but it had been moved before I got here.
(HOLMES *kneels and turns back the sheet, examining
the body keenly in the region of the heart.*)

HOLMES. Undoubtedly killed by a single revolver bullet.
(*He takes out his magnifying glass and looks intently
at the chest.*)
Fired from at least four metres away.
(*He looks up at* FORRESTER.)

FORRESTER. How's that, sir?

HOLMES. No powder-blackening on the clothing.
(FORRESTER *scratches his head.* HOLMES *replaces the
sheet and straightens up.*)
Inspector, will you show me the spot where the mur-
derer escaped over the hedge?
(FORRESTER *indicates the extreme R. of the stage.*)

FORRESTER. Just over here, sir. The Cunninghams both
pointed it out exactly.
(HOLMES *moves to where he has indicated and bends,
hands on knees, to scrutinize the ground.*)

HOLMES. Hm! One or two boot-marks . . . Let me see
your soles, please.
(FORRESTER *raises one of his boot-soles for inspection.*
HOLMES *nods.*)
I expected as much. Otherwise . . . nothing.
(*He straightens up and stands staring down at the
ground, puffing his pipe thoughtfully.*)

FORRESTER. What do you make of it, Mr. Holmes?
(*They move back to mid-stage.*)

HOLMES. Inspector, may I see that piece of paper again?

FORRESTER. Certainly, sir. (*He hands it to* HOLMES.)

HOLMES (*after a moment*). I think we're both agreed that

---

* **in situ**: on the spot

the finding of this in the dead man's hand is of extreme importance.

FORRESTER. Well, it *has* got "quarter to twelve" written on it—and that's almost the very moment he was killed.

HOLMES. Precisely. Whoever wrote that note was the man who brought William out of his bed at that hour. (*He holds up the torn fragment.*) But where is the rest of this sheet of paper?

FORRESTER. I searched everywhere for it.

HOLMES. It was torn out of the dead man's hand. Why was someone so anxious to get possession of it?

FORRESTER. Maybe it incriminated him.

HOLMES. Just so, inspector. And what would he do with it, having got it? He would most likely thrust it into his pocket, never noticing that a corner had been left in the grip of the corpse.

(*He puts the paper slowly into his pocket, as though it is an automatic movement.*)

FORRESTER. Very possible, Mr. Holmes.

HOLMES. Now, the man who wrote it wouldn't have written it at all if he could have delivered the message by word of mouth, would he?

FORRESTER. N-o.

HOLMES. So, who brought it? Or did it come through the post?

FORRESTER. Ah, that I can tell you, sir. We found out that William *did* get a letter by the afternoon post. No sign of the envelope anywhere, though.

HOLMES. Capital! Inspector Forrester, it's a pleasure to work with you. By the way, may I keep the piece of paper for the moment?

FORRESTER. If you wish, sir. Er, what about the body?

HOLMES. No, no. I fancy we have nothing more to learn from it.

(FORRESTER *gestures to the* CONSTABLES, *who pick up the stretcher and bear the body off R.* HAYTER *and* WATSON *enter R. at that moment, hastily removing their hats and standing respectfully as the body passes.*)

WATSON. Holmes, how're you feeling?

HOLMES. Never better, my dear fellow.

HAYTER. Found out anything yet?

HOLMES. Yes, Colonel—that this crime is a very peculiar one. Perhaps our visit to the Cunninghams' may do something to make it less obscure.

HAYTER (*glancing past him to Stage L.*). Well, here they are.

(CUNNINGHAM *and* ALEC CUNNINGHAM *enter L.* HAYTER *moves to shake hands and introduce them.*) Cunningham, me dear chap—and Alec, me boy. So sorry about all this. Terrible, terrible. Er, meet Mr. Sherlock Holmes and Dr. Watson.

(*handshakes exchanged and ad lib* greetings*)

CUNNINGHAM. Well, Mr. Holmes, we've heard of you— even in these parts.

ALEC. You don't mean to say the Inspector's called you in for anything straightforward as this?

HOLMES. Hardly straightforward, I think.

CUNNINGHAM. Ah! Then you've found some sort of clue?

FORRESTER. In a way, sir. You see, there was a . . .

(*He breaks off as* HOLMES *gives a loud groan and faints at his feet.*)

Mr. Holmes!

WATSON. Great heavens, I might have expected it. Quickly, please, help me with him into the house.

---

* ad lib: dialogue made up by actors on stage

(*Between them they lift the unconscious* HOLMES *and carry him off L.*)

SCENE THREE

(*The Cunningham's parlour. A window* (*optional*) *is in the back wall. The room has an untidy air, with things littered about—walking sticks in a stand, a pair of boots, a chair with a deed-box and documents on it. Slightly to R. is a sofa or chaise-longue on which* HOLMES *lies, head back and eyes closed, his feet in the direction of stage L. Near the foot of the sofa is a small table on which stands a carafe of water. At L., an old dressing-gown hangs on a hat-stand or hook. Near to it is another small table on which are a lamp and some papers and a pencil. The* CUNNINGHAMS, FORRESTER, *and* HAYTER *are standing behind and around the sofa, looking down at* HOLMES. WATSON *hovers near his head with a glass of water ready.* HOLMES *groans and stirs.*)

ALEC. He's coming to.

(WATSON *moves quickly to* HOLMES *and assists him as he struggles to sit up.*)

WATSON. Easily, Holmes. Lie still for a bit.

HOLMES (*weakly*). Watson?

WATSON. A sip of water?

(HOLMES *nods.* WATSON *holds the glass while he sips from it, then hands it to* FORRESTER, *who replaces it on the small table beside the carafe. They look on as* HOLMES *brushes his hand across his eyes, shakes his head to clear it, and, with* WATSON'S *aid, wriggles into a half-sitting position.*)

No hurry, Holmes. Just take your time.

HAYTER. You, er, feeling all right now, old chap?

HOLMES (*with an effort*). Thank you, Colonel. Gentlemen, I can't apologize enough.

CUNNINGHAM. Not at all.

HOLMES. These confounded nervous attacks. So suddenly . . .

CUNNINGHAM. Yes, yes. Dr. Watson's been telling us how ill you've been.

WATSON. *And* how you won't listen to common sense, Holmes. The sooner you're back at Hayter's, and in bed, the better.

(HOLMES *nods weakly and shuts his eyes.*)

CUNNINGHAM. Look here, I'll call my carriage to take you back.

HOLMES. Perhaps in a little while.

WATSON. *Now,* Holmes.

HOLMES (*rather slyly*). No—since I'm here, there is one little point I might as well verify.

(WATSON *and* HAYTER *exchange significant glances.*)

I should like to ask Mr. Cunningham Junior what he was doing when he heard William call for help?

ALEC. I've told the Inspector—I was sitting smoking in here. I always do, last thing—wearing that disreputable old dressing-gown, I'm afraid. (*pointing apologetically to it and grinning*)

HOLMES. By lamplight?

ALEC. Of course.

HOLMES. Doesn't it strike you as extraordinary that a burglar should break into a house when lights were on and the family might still be afoot?

CUNNINGHAM. Bit of a cool customer, perhaps.

HOLMES. Possibly. Mr. Cunningham, there is something I should like you to do.

CUNNINGHAM. Anything at all.

HOLMES. I should like you to offer a reward, which I will

arrange to have published. If you have a pencil and paper, by any chance? . . .

(ALEC *picks them off the table with the lamp and hands them to* HOLMES.)

Thank you.

(*He writes.*)

Fifty pounds would be quite enough, I think.

(*He hands the paper to* CUNNINGHAM.)

If you wouldn't mind reading it and signing it?

(CUNNINGHAM *reads.*)

CUNNINGHAM. Yes, this is all right. But there's one little mistake. You begin (*reads*) "Whereas, at about a quarter to one on Tuesday morning, an attempt was made . . . et cetera, et cetera." Well, it was a quarter to twelve.

HOLMES. Dear me, of course you're right. I don't allow myself to make such elementary mistakes.

(*He offers the pencil to* CUNNINGHAM, *who takes it and alters the incorrect word.*)

CUNNINGHAM. It's right now.

(*He hands the paper back to* HOLMES, *who glances at it and pockets it.*)

HOLMES. Thank you. And now, Watson, I surrender to your charge.

WATSON. And about time too.

(WATSON *moves to assist* HOLMES, *who rises and leans slightly on his friend's arm. They walk slowly towards L. When they reach the table on which the carafe and glass stand,* HOLMES, *shielded from the others' view by* WATSON, *who does not see what he does, deliberately upsets it.*)

HOLMES. Oh, Watson! What a clumsy fellow you are!

WATSON. I! Holmes . . .

HOLMES. Quickly—the carpet.

WATSON. Well, really, I . . .

(*He turns, pulling out his handkerchief to begin dabbing at the carpet. The others cluster round him, picking up the table and the broken glass. Unnoticed,* HOLMES *darts across to the dressing-gown and rummages in its pockets.*)

CUNNINGHAM. Think nothing of it, Dr. Watson. Water won't do any harm.

(ALEC *glances up and sees* HOLMES. *He hesitates for a moment.*)

WATSON. I really can't think how it happened . . .

(HOLMES *draws a piece of crumpled paper from the dressing-gown pocket.*)

ALEC (*urgently*). Father!

(CUNNINGHAM *looks up, follows his son's gaze and sees* HOLMES *beginning to straighten out the paper.*)

CUNNINGHAM. Now, sir, this is going too far.

ALEC. Give me that.

(*He hurries to* HOLMES, *who is reading the paper, and tries to snatch it.* HOLMES *eludes him.* ALEC *grapples with him.*)

HAYTER. I say, Alec! Cunningham!

CUNNINGHAM (*fiercely*). Keep out of this!

(*He goes to help his son.* HOLMES *holds the paper high above his head, out of their reach, as they struggle with him.*)

WATSON. Holmes . . .

HOLMES. Inspector—arrest these men.

FORRESTER. Arrest? . . .

HOLMES. For the murder of William, their coachman.

CUNNINGHAM. He's mad.

(WATSON, HAYTER, *and* FORRESTER *have moved to try to separate them. There is a general hubbub.*)

HAYTER. Another breakdown, Watson?

WATSON (*grimly, now struggling in earnest with* CUN-
NINGHAM). I don't think so.

HOLMES. Quickly, Forrester—before they can snatch this
paper. It's our vital evidence.

(**FORRESTER** *blows his whistle.* ALEC *breaks away and
tugs a revolver from his pocket.* WATSON *leaps across
to seize his arm and force it down. The revolver fires
into the floor.* WATSON *wrenches* ALEC's *arm and the
weapon falls from his hand.* WATSON *puts his foot on
it. The two* CONSTABLES *run in R. and secure* ALEC
and CUNNINGHAM, *indicated by* FORRESTER.)

FORRESTER. Right. That's enough from you two.

HOLMES. Thank you, Inspector.

FORRESTER. Thank *you,* Mr. Holmes. I've seen enough to
justify an arrest, though what your evidence is, I'll
have to hear later. (*to the prisoners*) Come on, gentlemen.

(*The* CONSTABLES *urge them towards R.*)

HOLMES. A moment. I should like Mr. Cunningham, or
his son, to confirm one thing for me.

ALEC. You'll get nothing from me, Holmes.

HOLMES. I *am* right in thinking that William was blackmailing you both?

ALEC. Think what you like!

CUNNINGHAM. No, Alec. (*wearily*) Yes, Mr. Holmes.
You're right.

HOLMES. Thank you. That will be all.

(**FORRESTER** *signs to the* CONSTABLES *and follows them
as they march the prisoners off R.*)

HAYTER. Blackmail, Holmes? Blackmail? How on earth
d'you know that?

(**HOLMES** *walks rather wearily to the chaise-longue and
reclines on it again. He takes from his pocket the original fragment of paper and fits it to the larger one.*)

HOLMES. Have a look at this.

(*They go round behind the chaise-longue and peer over his shoulder.*)

Don't you observe something very revealing about it?

HAYTER. Can't say I do.

WATSON. Pretty irregular sort of handwriting.

HOLMES. Exactly, Watson. Of course, he is better up in my methods than you, Colonel. No, there cannot be the least doubt that this note was written by two persons.

WATSON. Two!

HOLMES. Doing alternate words.

HAYTER. By Jove, you're right! But what on earth for?

HOLMES. Obviously one mistrusted the other. The idea was that each of them should have an equal part in the business. Of the two, I should say that the ringleader was the man who wrote "at" and "to" and "learn," et cetera.

HAYTER. However can you say that?

HOLMES. If you look closely, you'll see that those words were obviously written first, and blanks were left for the other writer to fill in. But they weren't always big enough. Look how the second man had to squeeze to get the word "quarter" in between the "at" and the "to."

WATSON. Bravo, Holmes!

HAYTER. Magnificent bit of deduction!

HOLMES. But very superficial. You may not know that the deduction of a man's age from his writing has been brought to considerable accuracy by experts. In this case, looking at the bold, strong hand of the one writer, and the rather broken-backed appearance of the other, we can say that the former was a young man and the latter was advanced in years.

HAYTER. Well, I never heard anything to touch this. Did you read anything *else* in the handwriting?

HOLMES. Oh yes. There were at least twenty-three other deductions . . .

HAYTER. Twenty! . . .

HOLMES. But they would be of more interest to experts than to you, Colonel—except, perhaps, that some of them reveal quite clearly that the two writers were blood-relatives.

(HAYTER *and* WATSON *laugh.*)

WATSON. How did you connect this with the Cunninghams, Holmes?

HOLMES. Oh, that came to my mind almost as soon as I saw the bullet wound in the dead man. There was no powder-blackening on the clothes, so the shot must have been fired from at least four metres away. Yet Alec Cunningham had told the Inspector he saw William and his attacker at grips with one another at the time.

(HOLMES *gets up and prowls about.*)

At the place where the Cunninghams had stated the murderer escaped across the hedge, the ground was soft enough to show impressions of the Inspector's boots—yet there were no traces of any others. I was not only sure that both the Cunninghams had lied, but also that there had been no unknown man on the scene at all.

HAYTER. Then, you mean to say that one of them shot William?

HOLMES. Alec, at a guess.

HAYTER. But why?

HOLMES. I thought back at once to what you had told me about a burglary at the house of your friend Mr. Acton. What did you say was missing?

HAYTER. Er, pair of candlesticks, ivory letter-weight, small barometer, ball of twine, . . .

HOLMES. And a copy of the *Odyssey*. A strange selection of loot, wouldn't you agree?

HAYTER. Hardly worth the risk.

HOLMES. Precisely. It seemed to be obvious that the burglars had been after something else, had failed to find it, so had swept a few things into their bag to make their search look like an ordinary burglary.

WATSON. Hayter, didn't you say there'd been a long lawsuit between Acton and the Cunninghams?

HAYTER. Going on for years.

WATSON. Then, it's my bet the Cunninghams did the burglary themselves. They were after some document without which Acton couldn't hope to win the case.

HOLMES. Capital, Watson! My reading entirely.

WATSON. Wait, Holmes. Their coachman, William, knew what they'd tried to do, and started blackmailing them. He'd be on his guard against them, so they concocted that note, as though it was from some stranger, to lure him into the grounds that night and murder him in a way no one could connect with them.

HOLMES. Magnificent! Watson, you're a credit to my training.

WATSON. Thank you. But I still don't see . . .

HOLMES. Dear me!

WATSON. I don't see how you knew where to find that other piece of paper that would prove all this. I mean, without that you could only assume they were guilty.

HOLMES. Quite true. I had to find the missing part of the note in the possession of one of them. I was certain that Alec must have torn it from the dead man's hand. He was wearing his dressing-gown at the time, I'd been told.

(*He takes the dressing-gown from its hook and fondles it.*)

Ten to one he'd have thrust the paper unthinkingly into its pocket. I wanted badly to see that dressing-gown, but Inspector Forrester nearly ruined everything for me.

(FORRESTER *enters briskly R.*)

FORRESTER. What's this, Mr. Holmes? Fair play, now!

HOLMES. When the Cunninghams joined us outside the house, you started to tell them about the one clue we'd found—that torn piece of paper in the dead man's hand. If you'd been allowed to finish, Alec would certainly remember the other piece in his dressing-gown pocket and hurry in here to destroy it. But, by the luckiest chance in the world, I, er, tumbled down in some sort of faint.

(*He tosses the dressing-gown to* FORRESTER *who catches it, astonished.*)

FORRESTER. You . . . you mean to say you were bluffing!

WATSON (*laughing*). Holmes, in all my years of practice I've seen plenty of fellows collapse at my feet, but I don't mind admitting you took me in.

HOLMES. Oh, it's an art I often find useful. Well, when I'd, er, recovered I managed by some little ingenuity to get old Cunningham to change the word "one" to "twelve" on that reward notice, so that I could compare his writing of "twelve" with the "twelve" in the original note.

HAYTER. And all this happened before our eyes. What a blind idiot I've been!

HOLMES. Then, by contriving to upset that carafe . . .

WATSON. You see! I knew *I* hadn't knocked the blessed thing over!

HOLMES. . . . I managed to divert attention long enough to search the dressing-gown pockets and find what I wanted. (*yawns*) Alec saw that the game would be up in a moment, hence his recourse to violence. (*yawns*) Oh, dear me!

(*He goes back to the chaise-longue and stretches out on it.*)

Watson, you should have reminded me that I'm an invalid.

(**WATSON** *rolls his eyes helplessly.* **HOLMES** *lays back his head and shuts his eyes.*)

FORRESTER. Just a minute, Mr. Holmes. There are a lot of details I want to hear from you.

HOLMES (*eyes shut, yawning*). Apply to Watson. He will embellish the narrative with far more colour than I should give it.

(**WATSON** *gives* **HOLMES** *a hard look, then takes the dressing-gown from* **FORRESTER** *and drapes it across* **HOLMES'** *body, picking up the paper as he does so. He beckons* **FORRESTER** *over to L.,* **HAYTER** *following, and shows him the paper.*)

WATSON (*quietly*). First of all, Inspector, have a look at this. Don't you observe something very revealing about the handwriting?

(**FORRESTER** *stares at* **WATSON**, *scratching his head. The curtain falls slowly as* **WATSON** *continues.*)

Now, to an expert, there can be no possible doubt that this note was written by two persons, doing alternate words. If you'll look closely it'll be quite obvious to you that one of them was elderly and one young, and which of them was the ringleader. You see how one left blanks for the other to fill in, and . . .

About the Authors

Novelist, activist, and educator **Isabel Allende** was born in Lima, Peru, in 1942. Allende has travelled and worked in South America, where many of her critically acclaimed novels are set.

Karleen Bradford discovered children's literature when she became a mother, and has been writing her own stories since then. Born in Toronto, she has lived in South America, North America, England, Southeast Asia, and Germany.

Elizabeth Brewster was born in Chipman, New Brunswick, in 1922. She is a respected poet, short-story writer, and novelist.

Jan Harold Brunvand is a professor of English and folklore at the University of Utah and was born in 1933. He has published several books of urban legends and writes a syndicated newspaper column about stories he has heard.

Once a teacher, **Charles Causley** is now an award-winning poet. His writing career began early; he started a novel when he was nine years old. Causley has also written three one-act plays and a Victorian comedy.

Margaret Clark was born and grew up in Darlington, England. Clark worked in the publishing business throughout her professional life, until she retired in 1988. This story is from her book *The Best of Aesop's Fables*.

More than sixty years after **Sir Arthur Conan Doyle**'s death (1859–1930) his fictional creation, Sherlock Holmes, lives on. Conan Doyle wrote many detective stories featuring Holmes and his sidekick, Doctor Watson. Many of these stories have been adapted as plays and films.

Stanley Cook lives in Yorkshire, England, where he writes poetry for young people ages four and older. Cook has published several collections of poetry, and many of his poems have been read on radio programs in England.

Poet, critic, and professor **Elizabeth Cook-Lynn** is a Crow Creek Sioux. She was born in 1930.

Born in London in 1925, **John Cotton** was a headmaster of a British school for twenty-two years. He has published numerous collections of poetry, and much of his work is also featured in anthologies.

Jennifer Currie was a student at Moscrop Secondary School in Burnaby, British Columbia, when she wrote this story. The piece won honourable mention in a British Columbia English Teachers' Association contest, and was published in the Association's *Student Writing Journal 1991–1992*.

Gabriel García Márquez began his writing career as a newspaper reporter in Colombia, where he was born in 1928. His novel *One Hundred Years of Solitude* brought him international acclaim and won the 1982 Nobel Prize in literature.

Writer **Mona Gardner** (1900–1981) published numerous novels and short stories. She lived in Hong Kong, South Africa, and California.

Michael and **Mollie Hardwick** met each other while working for the British Broadcasting Corporation drama department. They became a writing team best known for their novelizations—books created from movies and television series. They also wrote a series of theatrical adaptations of Sir A. Conan Doyle's Sherlock Holmes stories.

Jamaica Kincaid was born in 1949 in the West Indies. Her stories, many of which describe her girlhood in Antigua, were originally published in magazines. They later formed the basis for her celebrated novels.

Gordon Korman, born in Montréal in 1963, was twelve years old when he wrote his first book as a grade seven English assignment. Many of his books have won awards in Canada and the United States.

Ursula K. Le Guin was born in Berkeley, California, in 1929. She has written numerous novels, which are labeled science fiction but also concentrate on social and personal issues. Le Guin has led international writing workshops and has received many honours for her writing.

Jay Macpherson teaches English at the University of Toronto. She writes literary criticism and studies folklore, mythology, and history. Born in 1931, she has also published several books of poetry.

Marie Anne McLean is a storyteller as well as an elementary school teacher and librarian. She learned the art of storytelling from her family and usually writes about the real-life events and people of Saskatchewan, which is her current home.

Tololwa M. Mollel wrote, directed, and acted in his first play when he was in grade twelve in Tanzania. A doctoral student at the University of Alberta, he has taught there as well as at the University of Dar es Salaam in Tanzania. "The Orphan Boy" is the first of many stories he has published.

Raised in Harlem in New York City, **Walter Dean Myers** writes books about the positive experiences of children and teenagers who live in difficult environments.

Phyllis Reynolds Naylor (born in 1933) has written many books, four of them set at her grandparents' house in Maryland. She has been a full-time writer since 1960, and is active in civil rights and peace organizations.

Richard Peck has written many young adult novels about controversial topics. His stories, three of which have been made into television movies, reflect the issues he observed as a high school teacher. Peck was born in 1934 and lives in New York City.

Ruth Roston was born in Illinois, and did not begin writing poetry until the age of fifty-three. Her poems have appeared in many magazines and anthologies, and she has published a collection of her work.

Saki is the pen name of British writer Hector Hugh Munro, who was born in Akyab, Myanmar (formerly Burma), in 1870. He wrote scores of short stories, including a series about two young heroes who merrily take revenge on the adult world.

Amy Tan was born in California in 1952 after her parents came to the United States from China. She has written several award-winning novels.

Julie V. Watson has written seven books, and is considered one of Prince Edward Island's best-known authors. The story printed here is from *Ghost Stories & Legends of Prince Edward Island*.

Jordan Wheeler was born in 1964 in Victoria of Cree, Ojibway, Irish, English, Scottish, and French descent. He began writing at the age of seventeen, and has published several stories. He also works in video, film, and popular theatre with inner-city youth from Winnipeg. He and his wife, Tanis, have two children, Cam and Kaya.

Credits

Grateful acknowledgment is given to authors, publishers, and agents for permission to reprint the following copyrighted material. Every effort has been made to determine copyright owners. In the case of any omissions, the Publisher will be pleased to make suitable acknowledgments in future editions.

1 From *Traditional Chinese Folktales* by Yin-lien C. Chin, Yetta S. Center, and Mildred Ross. Copyright © 1989 by M.E. Sharpe, Inc. Published by M.E. Sharpe, Inc.

11 "Secretly" by Ruth Roston. Reprinted by permission of the author.

13 Reprinted from CURSES! BROILED AGAIN! THE HOTTEST URBAN LEGENDS GOING, by Jan Harold Brunvand, by permission of W.W. Norton & Company, Inc. Copyright © 1989 by Jan Harold Brunvand.

16 From *Ghost Stories & Legends of Prince Edward Island* by Julie V. Watson. Copyright © 1988 by Julie V. Watson. Reprinted by permission of the author.